Fairy Tales
IN THE classroom

*Teaching Students to Write Stories with
Meaning Through Traditional Tales*

D0731602

Veronika Martenova Charles
Foreword by Betsy Hearne

Fitzhenry & Whiteside

Fairy Tales in the Classroom:
Teaching Students to Create Stories with
Meaning Through Traditional Tales

Fitzhenry and Whiteside Limited
195 Allstate Parkway
Markham, Ontario L3R 4T8

In the United States:
311 Washington Street,
Brighton, Massachusetts 02135

www.fitzhenry.ca   godwit@fitzhenry.ca

Fitzhenry & Whiteside acknowledges with thanks the Canada Council for the Arts,
and the Ontario Arts Council for their support of our publishing program.
We acknowledge the financial support of the Government of Canada through the
Book Publishing Industry Development Program (BPIDP) for our publishing activities.

National Library of Canada Cataloguing-in-Publication
Charles, Veronika Martenova
Fairy tales in the classroom : teaching students to create stories with meaning
through traditional tales / Veronika Charles ; introduction by Betsy Hearne.
Includes bibliographical references and index.
ISBN 978-1-55455-020-3
1. English language—Composition and exercises—Study and teaching (Elementary).
2. Creative writing (Elementary education). 3. Fairy tales.
I. Title.
LB1576.C467 2009   372.62'3044   C2009-902082-3
United States Cataloguing-in-Publication Data is available from the Library of Congress.
Cover and interior design by Tanya Montini
Cover photo by David Orin Charles
Cover illustrations and interior illustrations are the property of the author.
Printed and bound in Hong Kong, China

1 3 5 7 9 10 8 6 4 2

Foreword
by Betsy Hearne

Once upon a time, every culture in the world depended on the oral tradition to express its literature, history, and beliefs. Storytellers used narrative patterns to help them remember long passages and complex plots. Family storytellers passed on tales honed through generations, with characters reflecting heroism, villainy, generosity, greed, benevolence, envy, trust, and trickery. Out of this vast body of folklore emerged certain story patterns, or "tale types," that became recognizable despite details that varied from culture to culture. Most of us know the basic storyline of "Cinderella," for instance, a common tale type that we share—in varied form—with other peoples worldwide.

Since the invention of printing, we have relied on books to store knowledge beyond the capacity of human memory, and the electronic age compounds that trend by multiplying our sources and quantities of information. And yet we still tell stories. Folklore persists in all our families and communities, though it's often unrecognized as coming from the same pools of imagination and experience as did folk and fairy tales. At parties, over the dinner table, in the playground and at the workplace, young and old tell stories of triumph and disaster on a daily basis. These stories are often fragmentary and disorganized compared to the tales that have survived over centuries, but still they have meaning and impact. The instinct for storytelling is alive, and Veronika Charles's book *Fairy Tales in the Classroom* bridges the worlds of old and new storytelling, of listening and retelling, of the oral and the written experience.

Children are naturally captive to the power of story in all forms. Those of us who work with them have abundant anecdotal evidence of this. They are magnetically drawn to narrative patterns that order the chaotic universe in which they seek to survive and gain some control. They often demand the same story over and over when it satisfies some unspoken need, and surprisingly, they still respond to the simple human interaction of tale and teller without pictures, costumes, or special effects. During the many years that I taught storytelling and folklore to university students who would become librarians and teachers, this trust in the power of imaginative listening was the first and hardest lesson they had to learn (an educational journey that I partially describe in a 2005 *Horn Book* article called "The Bones of Story"). What convinced them was their own class experience of going back to the basics of storytelling, learning but not memorizing the motifs of a story, and holding their classmates riveted by their own re-creation of it. They had to let go their fear of "doing it wrong" and find a balance between retaining the pattern that originally held the story together and incorporating their own new interpretation of it. Barre Toelken calls this balance of tradition and innovation the "dynamics of folklore," and it's a process that keeps any story alive and relevant to a changing society. Time and again, these students were further convinced by testing their storytelling with children in schools and public libraries set among multicultural populations.

Two exercises effectively prepared these students to tell their stories without memorization or props. The first involved stripping a simple folktale like "The Gunniwolf" to its basic elements (a little girl defies her mother's warning, ventures into the forest, meets a wolf, and tricks him into letting her get safely back home) and then retelling it as a class, with each student adding a sentence or two to what happens in the story; this built an immediate sense of community and relief from individual performance anxiety. The second exercise involved examining a more complex fairy tale such as "Beauty and the Beast" for its basic elements, reading variants from many different cultures in an anthology *(Beauties and Beasts)* that I edited during my several decades of studying the tale, and then breaking into groups. Each group recreated the tale in a different setting, from inner city to futuristic world, with different details, and told its version to the others. They re-contextualized a text according to their own imaginative play.

In addition to the practice of storytelling, we discussed theories and interpretations of folk and fairy tales—including those highlighted here in Veronika Charles's book—by the structural folklorist Vladimir Propp, the Freudian analyst Bruno Bettelheim, the Jungian psychologist C.G. Jung, the linguist and fantasy writer J.R.R. Tolkien, the Marxist-feminist critic Jack Zipes, and several theorists of children's relationship with stories, including Arthur Applebee, André Favat, and Gianni Rodari. Thus, when I read the manuscript for *Fairy Tales in the Classroom* and found Charles applying these landmark ideas to an impressive study involving more than 700 students in 23 classrooms in 15 schools of diverse racial and socioeconomic backgrounds, I was struck by what a uniquely valuable body of evidence she has provided for all of us who explore the relationship of children and story. The gift she has bestowed on us is twofold. First, she introduces and synthesizes, for   anyone without a folkloric background, selected theories on folk and fairy tales that, in spite of critical challenges to their validity, have influenced our thinking. More important, she puts these theories into practice with an extensive and systematic research project that proves how effective folk and fairy tales can be when used as creative springboards into writing, art, and other areas of the curriculum.

Charles's style is personable as she takes us through her journey from a childhood passion for fairy tales in her native Czechoslovakia through a quest for knowledge that brought her to this remarkable project. She is eloquent on the value of fairy tales as a genre for children of many socio-economic, cultural, and language backgrounds:

> "At the heart of the fairy tale is the idea that nothing we do is ever lost—the idea of the indestructibility of our acts. We learn that a jewel thrown into the sea, a kindness to an injured bird, a greeting to a stranger all have some intrinsic value and will have an effect on the destiny of all of us. Everything and everyone in the world are connected." (p. 12).

Charles is also persuasive in demonstrating the way children exercise their imaginations in response to hearing a tale, grasping its basic elements through interactive guidance and reconstructing a story of their own based on these elements, but more reflective of, and relevant to, their own experience.

> "The class preparation for the creation of a new story should consist solely of listening to the sample tale. It establishes the mood and casts its spell over the audience. It activates the right side of the brain, which deals with feelings and instincts. Perhaps listening to a story first is what opens the psyche of the audience who become more attuned to the next step, the creation of a new story. In other words, *listening* acts as a limbering-up exercise before the dance. When the children are then asked for their ideas *during* the creation of a new story, that is, while they are immersed in the moment, they respond to what has gone on before instinctively because the story itself leads them on." (p. 92)

Just as impressive as her examples of the children's fairy tale versions is her inclusion and thoughtful analysis of the vivid pictures they made to illustrate them. The evidence of her program's success is irrefutable and the selection of fairy tales used to springboard into the children's creative work is unusual, with an international scope. Teachers are provided with clear footprints to follow for experimentation of their own; even if they don't use a strictly Proppian form of analysis, this system will work. Since reading aloud, as Charles suggests, is less daunting than "learning" a story to tell, there is no barrier to adopting a practice with so many possibilities of classroom enrichment.

In a world filled with distracting multimedia, it is difficult to give children the time and space for focused concentration. Quite beyond the messages of strength and survival that folktales provide is the space they give for each of us to listen between the lines and to order our own universe according to individual understanding. We can color the characters' skins, as did the children in this study, whatever color we are. We can see ourselves as heroes or helpers, project the faces of villains and victims we know onto those of the tale. From the logic of cause and effect to the expansion of a narrative vocabulary to fit new situations, listening to and reconstructing fairy tales contributes to coherence in children's learning and in their lives. This book offers an irresistible place to start.

Betsy Hearne,
Professor Emerita, University of Illinois, Urbana-Champaign

Table of Contents

What Can I Write About?

Children often ask, "What can I write about?" when their teacher asks them to write a story in class. The blank piece of paper lies in front of them, but they don't know how to start. I hear a similar question when I go to schools as a visiting author and talk to children about my books and what it is like to write them. "Where do you get your ideas from?" the children ask me.

"Well," I respond, "when I was little, I listened to many fairy tales. Now, I get ideas from everything around me, and I do a lot of daydreaming."

"What is daydreaming?" the children ask.

This question about daydreaming made me pause and think about how much things have changed in the course of just one generation. Today, children are bombarded by media: television, the Internet, and video games in particular. Electronic media demand fast reaction; there is no time allowed to stop and reflect on the situation. There is no time for daydreaming.

Many teachers comment about how today's students seem not to respond to verbal instructions as well as students of the previous generations. The Twenty-first Century's children, however, are a product of our culture, and they process information differently. The continually shifting images and sound bytes of our visual culture have created visual learners. No wonder they have a short attention span and crave instant gratification. Today, many children lead hectic and stressful lives.

When I think back to my own childhood, I remember how often fairy tales comforted me in times of stress. How I wish that I could give children back those tales, not the animal fables or the sanitized Disney versions, but the other, lesser-known ones that I found so compelling. Perhaps they could help relieve some of the pressure and anxieties that today's children feel. After all, the fairy tales have served us that way for countless generations. But would today's children have the patience to read and listen to traditional stories that are text-heavy?

Curiosity and my desire to reconnect children with fairy tales led me to York University where I enrolled as a graduate student and embarked on a research study for my thesis. Was it possible to engage children with the stories so that they could take ownership and make them their own? Could it be done in the classroom? Could children get involved with the stories amid all the competition from the electronic and digital media that surround them? Could they adapt the stories and use them to deal with their own problems?

This book is about the unexpected discovery that emerged during my research and that took my breath away. I was astonished to witness how easily and quickly children can invent their own stories and how much writing they can do if they get involved in the stories personally.

Another finding that emerged totally unexpectedly and as a by-product of my research was that several children with autism or attention deficit disorder seemed, to the amazement of their teachers, to be reached by the method I used in the classroom. But before I go any further, let me first tell you a bit about myself and what brought me to write this book.

> *"I was astonished to witness how easily and quickly children can invent their own stories and how much writing they can do if they get involved in the stories personally."*

My own journey

I have had a lifelong love affair with fairy tales. They are infused in my blood. As a child, I listened to the tales on Czech radio's children's hour while playing near my mother who was sewing clothes. Then I made up my own stories modelled on the ones I heard, using buttons as the characters and moving them across landscapes I created out of fabric scraps. It felt good being in the stories' magic worlds where anything was possible and anything could happen. I could go into the imaginary places anytime and at my own will, play there, and then come back to the real world feeling exhilarated and happy.

To this day, the tales have a powerful hold on me. As long as I can feel enchanted by them, I know I'm truly alive. Looking back at my life, I can see how much it has been influenced by the tales I heard in my childhood. It seems as if I acted out the role of a fairy-tale heroine and followed in her footsteps, setting out alone on my journey into the world, going through a series of tests, and meeting helpful strangers along the way who, in times of need, assisted me and guided me along my journey. Life itself is a story.

Until I came to North America, I always thought that the fairy tales were a unique part of my Czech heritage, of the culture that bred me. So it came as a revelation to discover that in other places, in other languages, there were tales just like the ones I got to know as a child, and that similar tales existed all over the world. I came to realize that they were not a unique part of my Czech heritage but a common heritage of the human race. Even though the tales varied in details and settings, they were recognizable in their other guises. It did not seem to matter where the stories took place, who did what and under which circumstances; what seemed to matter was what really happened in those tales—in other words, the essence contained in their structural bones.

There is no original telling of fairy tales. They are the product of anonymous tellers, orally transmitted from generation to generation until fixed in print.

I first started writing stories in the form of lyrics for pop songs; later, I created my stories in the form of picture books. Somehow, the substance of the tales from my childhood would always come through and find its way into my writing. Some element of magic or perhaps a way of seeing the world around me would echo the old tales.

For instance, in my book *The Crane Girl* (1992), the common fairy-tale motif is metamorphosis. The heroine of the story feels rejected by her own family, but then is taken in by a family of cranes, and they transform her into one of their kind. The motif just came to me, unconsciously at first, because it was a part of what I knew—part of my stored-image vocabulary. Perhaps deep inside I needed to be connected again to those stories of my childhood. Or perhaps, because the stories were now part of me, I could not stop their elements from seeping into my own work. In any case, after I had done it, I realized that the idea of humans transforming into animals comes from fairy tales.

Suddenly, I became self-conscious and worried. I was afraid to admit that I had made the story up. My sense at the time was that since the "transformation" element had come from the fairy tale, I was not allowed to use it. When submitting it to a publisher, to justify my use of the folktale's motif, I pretended that I had heard the story from an old woman. The impression that folktales are untouchable because they are fixed in print is unfortunate, but common.

Another time, a story from my childhood just stayed with me and would not go away. Something about the story did not feel right, and there were questions prodding my mind that the story did not answer. The urge to tell the story from my point of view and to find the answer would not let go of me until I resolved it by creating my own tale.

That is how my book *Stretch, Swallow and Stare* (1999) came to be. The story sprouted from the seed of a Czech fairy tale of my childhood and then grew and blossomed on its own.

In the version I knew in my childhood, the characters were three male servants who, with their magical abilities, helped a prince free his bride from an evil wizard. In the story, the three characters appeared together halfway into the story. I always wanted to know how they met, where they came from. I tried to understand who the characters really were, and it seemed to me that their alienation and social rejection were a result of their "wrong" body types.

Because I could perceive them only from my present reality—our body-conscious, beauty-oriented culture—I decided they would best ring true if they were portrayed as women. So, in my version, three unusual female characters help a small boy in distress to search for his missing sister: "Stretch" is a tall woman who can make her body taller than a tree; "Swallow" is short and large and can eat a huge quantity of food; and "Stare" has eyes so powerful they burn through anything she looks at. It was then that the story took up a life of its own. It became the story of the search for their identity by three unusual heroines, who then find their place in the world by drawing strength from their uniqueness. It also became a story about female friendship, something that rarely appears in traditional tales.

In one of the schools I visited, the teacher-librarian used the story to create a project for her students. Using the book's basic plot line, the children created their own magical characters with special abilities, who win the contest with the evil wizard in the story. What a wonderful idea, I thought! The teacher-librarian gave the children permission to change the story and the opportunity to make it their own. Right there, the seed of my project was planted. Perhaps children could do this with traditional fairy tales, too. So many of these tales are gathering dust because they are filled with images and social values that no longer resonate with us.

Yes, fairy tales can be re-told and re-created. We own these stories and we not only can but we ought to make them reflect our present concerns and values and make them work for today's children as they have done for past generations.

Using fairy tales in the classroom

① Fairy tales are stories that particularly interest children between the ages of 6 and 8. Why not tap into what children love and respond to? In Chapter 3, I explain why children have such an interest in fairy tales.

② Fairy tales are a powerful tool for reflecting children's emotions. Children today face the same problems—for example, being held in low esteem, enduring sibling rivalry—as the heroes in fairy tales. Because these stories have a simple structure, they help children to sort out their feelings. In fact, the fantasy world can help children deal better with the real world (see Chapter 3).

③ Fairy tales help children acquire the "concept of story" as a coherent flow of events with a beginning, a middle, and an end. The ages of 6 to 8 seem to be the optimum time for children to internalize the narrative story structure, a pattern that can be established for life.

Like crawling before they walk and listening to language before they speak, absorbing the simple structure of fairy tales helps children firmly grasp the concept of story. Why? Fairy tales consist of sequences of actions linked together in a simple way by the words "and" or "then." Because action is what most interests children before the age of 10, children are attuned to it and can easily grasp the action patterns in stories.

④ Many outcomes or expectations expressed in the language arts curriculum at the primary level can easily be incorporated using the approach to fairy tales described in this book (see also Chapter 5).

⑤ My approach to fairy tales can also reach the difficult-to-reach children, such as those with autism or attention deficit disorder. How is that possible? Because the approach is interactive; my exploration of the fairy tale using graphic symbols, which I present in Chapter 4, engages them like video games. Also, my telling the story first reveals the goal before the steps leading up to the goal. Finally, by listening to the story without reading text or seeing illustrations, the children can visualize the story for themselves. These strategies were found to be effective in helping children with an attention deficit problem because these children are usually visual learners. [1]

⑥ Children gain a sense of empowerment by voicing their own ideas and by being listened to.

In upcoming chapters, I talk more in depth about fairy tales and children. By sharing my own work with you, I can show the remarkable results you can achieve when you connect the two through the method described in this book.

But, if you wish to get started right away, you can advance straight to Chapter 10, where you will find a brief description of the approach, followed by the anthology of fairy tales adapted, simplified, and tested in the classroom, and ready-to-use material for your work with students.

Why Fairy Tales Are Still with Us

There are countless books and studies devoted to the fairy tale genre. Fairy tales have been examined in the fields of history, anthropology, sociology, psychology, linguistics, and other disciplines. They have served as an inspiration for artists, poets, musicians, and filmmakers. The stories are still with us today, permeating our culture in various forms. Their motifs are used in advertisements, television commercials, marketing campaigns, and in some video games. Any parent or teacher can attest that the stories still hold children mesmerized.

What are fairy tales?

Fairy tales are stories about ordinary human beings and elements of magic. They are the products of anonymous tellers, orally transmitted from one generation to the next over the course of centuries until fixed in print. The name of the genre is misleading. The stories are not about fairies, diminutive creatures with fluttering wings, as the word "fairy" seems to suggest (although they do appear in some of the stories), but about *Faërie,* the realm in which fairies exist. In the Faërie realm there are witches, giants, dwarfs, and animals that speak. There is the sun, the moon and the wind, the sea and the mountain, the tree and the stone, water and bread. Among all this, mortals can be found when they are enchanted. J.R.R. Tolkien says that the definition of a fairy tale depends

> upon the nature of *Faërie:* the Perilous Realm itself, and the air that blows in that country. I will not attempt to define that, nor to describe it directly. It cannot be done. *Faërie* cannot be caught in a net of words; for it is one of its qualities to be indescribable, though not imperceptible.[2]

The Faërie realm lingers alongside the known human world, parallel to it yet separate. Just beyond our real-world periphery, it is like an extra dimension to our three-dimensional reality, something we cannot quite grasp but we know is there.[3] Perhaps the best way to define the stories would be as "wonder tales" because they awaken a sense of wonder in us and make us feel enchanted.

What does it mean to be enchanted? It seems to me that enchantment is a mental state in which we are filled with wonder and amazement, as when we see something for the very first time. It is the feeling that a small child has when discovering the world. G.K. Chesterton, the English novelist and literary critic, said,

> … when we are very young children … [M]ere life is interesting enough. A child of seven is excited by being told that Tommy opened a door and saw a dragon. But a child of three is excited by being told that Tommy opened a door.[4]

Perhaps this is how primordial humans saw the world before science set its foot in and started explaining everything in a factual manner. Then, there was no need for exaggeration or for fantasy because the world itself was mysterious, magical, and puzzling. Once the majority of humans separated themselves from nature, the wonder tales were created to remind them of the time when nature and mystery were perceived as one and as an expression of the deeply rooted "desire of men to hold communion with other living things."[5] Fairy tales restore in us that feeling of wonder, the enchantment with the natural world we once felt:

> These tales say that apples were golden only to refresh the forgotten moment when we found that they were green. They make rivers run with wine only to make us remember, for one wild moment, they run with water.[6]

If we willingly suspend disbelief and accept the magic in the story, for a moment we can remember what we had forgotten, who we really are, and feel at one with the cosmos. The acceptance of the story enables us to step outside of time and glimpse the memories of our ancestors.[7]

What is the significance of the tales?

That fairy tales are still around us is testimony to their relevance and power. They have survived because they are suffused with value for us and have spoken to us for centuries in different voices and with different levels of meaning.

Of all literature, fairy tales give the truest picture of life and of human destiny. Fairy tales are not concerned with the trivialities of particular moral codes; instead they contain elemental laws and ideals. One principal theme of the tales is the seeming disparity between appearances and reality. The least likely thing, for instance a wooden table or a walnut, turns out to be extraordinary upon a closer look. The least likely character, such as Simpleton or Cinderella, emerges as a hero. The tales tell us that our perceptions of things and of people do not necessarily reveal their true nature. To see truly, one has to look more deeply, to see under the exterior of things and of people. In fact, appearance and reality are what make a thing what it is, and the seeming disparity lies in our faulty perception. We tend to look for black and white where there are many shades of grey.

Thus, the principal theme of the tales is to see truly.[8] In the tales, the mundane and the magical are viewed as part of one another. Success is made to depend upon small, ordinary objects and observances, and life is presented as a chain of events. If a man touches three trees beside the road, he is safe; if he touches four, he loses everything he has. If he meets an old woman, he is to ask a particular question. If he picks a flower in the forest at the stroke of midnight, it will give him great powers. The sense of some small detail deciding our fate is genuine. None of us knows when we have done something irrevocable. Taking a different turn off the road or arriving someplace a few moments late may have decided our destiny.[9]

At the heart of the fairy tale is the idea that nothing we do is ever lost—the idea of the indestructibility of our acts. We learn that a jewel thrown into the sea, a kindness to an injured bird, a greeting to a stranger all have some intrinsic value and will have an effect on the destiny of all of us. Everything and everyone in the world are connected.

The stories tell us that all doors fly open to courage and hope. If the hero sets out into the world with desire and conviction, he will receive help along the way. We learn from the tales that, by loving a thing, we make it lovable. The stories tell us to be on guard against disguises and regard every repellent exterior with hopeful suspicion. Finally, we infer the principle central to the tales—that nothing can harm us unless we fear it. Therefore, we must face and defy the very thing that terrifies us.

The truth and value of the fairy tale arises from the total absence of the supernatural in the stories. It is a given that the real and fantastic co-exist on the same plane of human experience. There are no magic wands or crystal balls. The world itself is full of marvels and that is the way the hero or heroine perceives it.

The foundation for all of literature[10]

Fairy tales can be viewed as the "great-grandparents of narrative literature" to come.[11] As an archetypal form of literature, they initiate us into the experience of story. Their simple structures, absence of detailed characterization, but complex and emotionally loaded content make them a powerful tool for perception and reflection. The stories provide us with the experience of literature, while they encourage identification with the hero and the reading of oneself into the story's action. They provide space for the reader or listener to fill in the details and colour.[12]

The language of fairy tales is in the form of symbols, where everything means something more or something else. Because the tales contain archetypes, their meaning goes far beyond the words they contain, and they produce different meanings for every individual listener or reader. The meaning is likely to change for individuals, depending on their needs at the time. Perhaps each fairy tale can be viewed as a large buffet table, where the individuals pick what they are hungry for at the moment. These multiple meanings of the tales are imparted to us through the language of symbols, and they provide a safe initiation into the magic and mystery of life. They function as a mediator between ourselves and the world outside and help us to bring the two into accord.

A therapeutic value[13]

Recently, I met Bianca Molica Ganuza, a psychotherapist from Brazil, who works with terminally ill children in a hospital in São Paulo. She told me that when she gives the children a choice of things to do—

whether to play with toys, to draw, or to watch television, the only thing the dying children ask for is to listen to fairy tales.[14] They want to hear the same story over and over again, closing their eyes at the scary parts. Ganuza's account of these children reaching for the tales at the critical time in their lives is testimony to the power of the tales.

The power of the tales lies mainly in their language of metaphors and symbols. Such language is helpful when communicating with people in distress. In the Trauma Center at Harvard University, Dr. van der Kolk and his associates used brain imaging to study patients who were having flashbacks. They discovered that the right hemisphere of the brain (where images, vision, and emotions are located) was extremely active, while the left hemisphere of the brain (where speech and logic reside) was completely shut down, particularly the area that allows the patients to talk about their experiences. Metaphors and symbols are the language of the right hemisphere of the brain, which explains why fairy tales are helpful in therapy and why people are comforted by them at critical times of their lives.[15]

The essence of story[16]

An experience of story allows an individual to look at his own life as a story with a coherent flow of events. Through stories, particularly fairy tales, one acquires the experience of imaginative meaning that can be applied to one's life as a means of understanding and making sense of it. We are all the heroes of our own life stories. The fairy tales impart the sense of a complete human existence and reassure us that the journey through life, although filled with challenges and danger, can be wonderful.

Mining the potential of fairy tales

In the primary classroom, the fairy tale is one of the variety of literary texts read and discussed in the language arts; the stories can serve as a springboard for obtaining factual knowledge and exploring multiculturalism. For example, a teacher might read a fairy tale to the class and then deconstruct it, perhaps asking the children to identify patterns in the narrative, plot-carrying words, descriptive words, or concept-carrying words, or asking questions like, "When did you realize the problem in the story was solved?"

In teaching science or social studies, the teacher might read an African folktale and, while doing so, might display pictures of elephants, lions, and monkeys; link children's knowledge of wild animals to the story; locate Africa on the map, particularly the countries from which some of the students might have emigrated; measure the distances between them; and discuss the differences in their geography.

To expand their understanding of multiculturalism, the teacher might bring different versions of the same tale (Cinderella, for example) and ask the children to read them and make charts comparing the similarities and differences. The follow-up activities might include making costumes or dressing up like the characters in the tale, which has proven effective because children also enjoy working with these aspects of fairy tales.

Yet, there is an opportunity for students to get much more out of the stories if their minds are free to roam when allowed time for deeper reflection. If the nature of the activities following the reading or listening is of a suitable mode, the fairy tales can provide children with social and emotional guidance and with relief from the anxieties of daily life. They help students develop the inner resources to cope, to imagine other solutions, to think creatively when dealing with conflicts in the future.

Suitable follow-up activities would focus on the children's thoughts about the story and what personal experiences came to mind while listening to the reading, especially when these are discussed in an atmosphere of tentative mutual exploration. When the teacher's questioning enhances the children's experience of the story, they get more out of the tales and increase their understanding of themselves.[17]

There are some innovative programs in the educational landscape that use folk tales and fairy tales in a classroom setting, engaging children directly with the tales and promoting the use of their imagination. For instance, in Lynn Rubright's Project TELL, "Teaching English through Living Language," a fairy tale is used to motivate students to read and write and to make connections across different areas of the curriculum.[18] In Jack Zipes's "Neighbourhood Bridges," a storytelling and creative drama program, popular fairy tales provide a stage for practicing social awareness. Both programs are based upon principles similar to those in my work:

- The approach to fairy tales should be interactive through elements of play.
- Playing with the ancient narratives can help children become creative individuals and independent, innovative thinkers.

Such approaches pursue the meaning of *education,* which comes from the Latin root *educare* (or *educere*), meaning *to draw out from within.*[19] The focus of my own work is different from those in the two programs just mentioned, because I am concerned mainly with the relationship between children and stories. First, the relationship one has with the tale is essentially a private one. That relationship can be viewed as a dialogue between the essence of a person and the nucleus of the tale. Each individual has a unique dialogue with the tale. Second, as the tales are living entities, if one uses them, they should receive something back; they should be infused with new blood and new meaning from personal reflection; they should be recharged. The tales can provide a playground for the children, but the children have to go to the playground and engage in the play.

When children enter into the stories, play with them, and make the stories their own, they are able to rehearse their emotional responses within the secondary reality of the tales, thereby preparing themselves for real-life confrontations. By providing the opportunity for children between the ages of 6 and 8 to engage and interact with fairy tales on a reflective level, we can fully engage the children's imagination.

Going through the Fairy-Tale Woods

When I first embarked upon my journey to study fairy tales, I felt that I, myself, was crossing into a dark forest. Which way was the right way to go? Guided solely by my intuition at first, I found it exhilarating to come across the writings of the researchers and educators who had gone that way before me, and whose work then guided me further, like markers along the woodsy trail. Through their work, I could see that I was on the right track and that my intuition was correct.

These writings have been crucial to my study; many of the ideas contained in them are relevant to teaching in the primary classroom. Bruno Bettelheim tells us why fairy tales are nourishing and helpful to children. C.G. Jung illuminates what lies beneath the surface of the tales and tells what they are really about—the stages and trials encountered in human life. André Favat explains why children are so keenly interested in fairy tales and at which point in their development they could benefit most from the tales. Gianni Rodari shows how to help children exercise their imagination in response to the stories and how they can later apply what they learn to their own lives.

I can still remember the excitement I felt when I came across the work of the Russian linguist, Vladimir Propp, whose research confirmed what I had always instinctively felt—that it did not matter where the stories took place, who the characters were, or what they did, but rather it was what lay underneath that mattered; it was the structural bones of those stories that were of utmost importance. Propp picked those bones out, put them under the light, and identified them.

Toward the end of my exploration, I discovered the work of Arthur Applebee, whose observations on how children respond to stories at different developmental stages and how they construct stories themselves put the last piece of the puzzle in place for me.

What follows are my thoughts about the people whose work guided me on my journey, along with highlighted key ideas that could be directly applied to your teaching. They provide a deeper understanding of the fairy tale genre, with insight into how children relate to the stories. It is my hope that these ideas will further inspire you in your own work with children and fairy tales in the classroom.

Fairy Tales Are Good for Children

Bruno Bettelheim

A Freudian analyst and child psychologist, Bruno Bettelheim argues in his book *The Uses of Enchantment* that fairy tales are good for children because they nourish their inner feelings and help them deal with their emotions. Although the tales take place in the realm of fantasy, the heroes themselves are ordinary human beings who are confronted with family conflicts. The problems that these heroes face are the same today as they were hundreds of years ago: feelings of rejection, jealousy of their siblings, or being held in low esteem by their parents.

By projecting their own fears and wishes onto the fantasy figures in the tales, the children can sort out a range of conflicting emotions.

They need to distance themselves from their inner feelings and externalize them in order to gain some mastery over them. Because the fairy tale has a structure, a plot that moves forward, and a satisfying ending, it helps children order and clarify their feelings and relieve some of the pressures they feel.

When listening to a story in which the hero or heroine faces predicaments similar to their own, children are reassured to see this key figure resolve the problems in the fantasy world and return home victorious. The children can then hope that they, too, will get help when they need it and that they will find their place in the world. So the tales provide reassurance to children and promote their confidence in themselves and their future.

By following the journey of the tale's main character, noted Bettelheim, the children learn that permitting their fantasy to take hold of them for a while is not harmful as long as they don't get caught up in it permanently. Thus, the tales validate the children's inner experiences as worthwhile and legitimate, while they simultaneously provide guidance and suggest solutions to their problems. As Bettelheim expressed it, the adults who

> decided that if there were monsters in a story told to children, these must all be friendly … missed the monster a child knows best and is most concerned with: the monster he feels or fears himself to be, and which also sometimes persecutes him. By keeping this monster within the child unspoken of, hidden in his unconscious, adults prevent the child from spinning fantasies around it in the image of the fairy tales he knows. Without such fantasies, the child fails to get to know his monster better, nor is he given suggestions as to how he may gain mastery over it. As a result, the child remains helpless …[20]

Providing the opportunity within the school setting for children to engage with fairy tales, to have time for personal reflection and, through classroom discussions, to clarify the vocabulary for talking about their emotions is worthwhile. Engaging the children's active imagination with the tales helps establish patterns that, later on when the need arises, the children might access for their personal use.

Finding the Real World through the Magic Realm

C.G. Jung

Carl Jung was a Swiss psychologist, a colleague of Sigmund Freud and one of the founders of psychoanalysis. He has had a significant influence not only on psychology but also on philosophy and the arts. Through his interest in Eastern religions, mythology, and fairy tales, he inspired the New Age movement. Carl Jung is perhaps best known for his use of the term "archetype."[21]

In Jungian terms, archetypes are genetically inherited patterns of behaviour that reside in the psyche, resembling the instincts. They help us organize, understand, and make sense of the world around us. They bring what was previously hidden deep in our unconscious into our conscious mind to balance and unite all the elements in our psyche. This process of psychological growth can be understood as living life fully or coming into one's total identity.[22]

According to Jung, fairy tales mirror our psyche and describe the process of self-realization in its full complexity. They are told in the language of symbols, so they reach and open the deeper layers of our unconscious, stir emotions in us, and connect us with our imagination.

The characters in fairy tales can be seen as parts of one's personality. The hero, or the character with which we emotionally identify, represents the "ego"; the problem the character encounters can be viewed as the "complex" in the psyche. Just like the duality of the conscious and unconscious minds, there is a duality in the fairy tale, that is, the real world and the magic realm. The hero's crossing the threshold from reality into the magic realm, say, the dark forest, represents the ego entering the "unconscious." The journey that the hero undertakes symbolizes the ego's encounters with various archetypes. For example, the old man or the helpful animal that the hero meets in the magic realm and who provides him with much-needed help is the "spirit archetype," that is, the wisdom in the unconscious. The happy ending of the tale, in which the protagonist becomes king or queen and gets married, acts out the psychic growth of becoming a complete and balanced human being.

From such archetypes, countless symbols and images emerge. Symbols are only powerful and alive as long as they carry meaning. In the fixed, literal form of many fairy tales, quite a few of the symbols have lost their meaning because they were created by the culture of a particular time. For example, the terms "porridge" and "miller" are no longer widely recognized, so their power as symbols is diminished.

Jung says, "as each symbol and archetypal image formulation becomes obsolete, they require a new interpretation if they are not to lose their spellbinding power."[23] It would follow, then, that if fairy tales are to retain their potency, they have to be liberated from their fixed, literary form and recharged with new symbols and image-carrying meaning in order to speak to us in our contemporary world. To paraphrase the writer Susan Cooper, if the tales are like butterflies pinned at one moment in time, one should liberate them so that they can soar.

André Favat

André Favat was a researcher and an educator who received his Ph.D. in Education from Harvard University. He is best known for his book *Child and Tale: The Origins of Interest,* an extensive investigation of children's interest in fairy tales. In it, he juxtaposed the "children's psychological characteristics" with the "characteristics of the tales" to observe if and how they intersected in order to discover the cause of the interest.

For the "children's psychological characteristics," Favat drew on the early work of Jean Piaget.[24] For the "characteristics of the fairy tales," Favat used Propp's structural analysis. From the observation and comparison of both sets of characteristics, Favat concluded that fairy tales "embody an accurate representation of the child's conception of the world." The children's interest in fairy tales, as Favat notes, emerges around the age of 5, declines about the age of 10, with the highest point occurring between the ages of 6 and 8. That is the developmental stage when the children's characteristics mirror the characteristics of the fairy tales.

Belief in magic

One of their characteristics is the belief in magic. According to Piaget, children believe that all things are related and, if they "participate" with each other, reality can be altered. For instance, children believe that one object can influence another object; or that a particular action (such as jumping over sidewalk cracks) can influence an event that they wish for. The same relationship with magic exists in the world of the fairy tales. Objects, beings, actions, and thoughts exercise influence over each other, resulting in *magic*. For example, the hero needs only to wish for something and somehow the wish gets fulfilled.

The child also regards a large number of objects as living and conscious even if they don't move. For example, a stone may "feel" when it is touched and wood may "feel" burning when set on fire. In fairy tales, inanimate objects may move by themselves or speak with a human voice, and the appearance of speaking animals is common.

Children's moral world

The moral worlds of children parallel the moral worlds of fairy tales. Children accept prohibition from authority figures as absolute.[25] They do not see the actions in terms of inner motives or of their social meaning. Only the consequences determine the wrongfulness of the action.

In the tales as well, the laws are dictated by the "authorities"—the kings, fairy godmothers, and so on. To violate their laws or to break a promise made to the authorities means to violate the entire world order. Here, as well, the motivations and circumstances don't seem to matter. It is the action that matters, and it is judged by its result, not by the intention behind it.

Justice

In the child's perception, the way to set things right is through powerful punishment. Piaget's research showed that, to children at this developmental stage, justice is most "just" when it is most severe. There is no lack of powerful punishments in fairy tales; the villains often meet bizarre and violent deaths, which correspond with the child's view of punishment and justice.

Self-centredness

Another characteristic of children at this developmental stage is that they live under the impression that everyone shares their thoughts and desires. The fairy-tale hero moves the same way in his world, where all the forces seem to be operating on his behalf as he sets out to fulfill his desires.

When children retell stories, they stress the *events*, not their *causes* or the connection to the time in which they occur. The same could be said for the fairy tales, where mainly conjunctions such as "and" or "then" string the actions of the stories together without much concern for causes. Favat raises the point that perhaps it is the narrative structure of the tales, the stringing together of the events rather than the characters themselves, that is of real interest to the children.

From these comparisons, Favat was able to show that there is a precise correspondence between the child's perception and the fairy tale's universe. He then investigated what caused the intensity of interest in the tales and why children sought them out.

Source of comfort

As children mature into the next developmental stage, their psychological characteristics change. As their view of their world gets challenged, children become disoriented and they face crises when they try to readjust. But in fairy tales, Favat says, the children can get transported back into a familiar world, preserved and stable, which means that children turn to the tales for comfort and consolation. Children's hunger for the tales is a manifestation of their search for an ordered world they once knew, more satisfying than the real world in which they find themselves.

The fact that children seek the imaginary realm means that they recognize the two worlds. Shuttling back and forth between the real world and the imaginary world may be the source of pleasure and gratification, like sleep after a long day of labour. Just as sleep refreshes us and prepares us for the next day, the comfort provided by the story prepares the child to face the real world after the tale is over.

Favat's study indicates that children in this developmental stage are not likely to respond in the same way to realistic stories because these may add to the tensions and stresses the children already feel. Instead, we should provide children (between the ages of 6 and 8, in particular) the opportunity to interact with fairy tales because they are a source of comfort to them and because these are the stories that interest them the most.

One might argue that the Harry Potter phenomenon owes its success to our technology-driven culture because this culture has made us feel spiritually impoverished. It is quite possible that the curriculum's greater emphasis on reality, on fact-oriented education, deprives children of more opportunities to play, to daydream, and to imagine. Consequently, children are hungry for the magical.

Fairy Tale Form

Vladimir Propp

Vladimir Propp was a Russian linguist whose work *Morphology of the Folktale* is regarded as a major theoretical breakthrough in the study of folklore in the Twentieth Century. Propp viewed the folktale as a living organism. After analyzing one hundred Russian fairy tales, he concluded that all tales, no matter how different their characters or settings, contained the same basic structure. As Propp saw it, the structure consisted of a linear sequence of actions that he called "functions" which can be understood as a character's acts that, at a particular point in a story, move the plot forward. I will refer to them from now on as "actions."

Although the number of characters in fairy tales is varied and large, the number of actions the characters perform is quite small. To describe the form of the fairy tale, Propp defined 31 actions, and they are the stories' bones that I mentioned in this chapter's introduction.

Propp's 31 Actions

For your work in the classroom, you do not have to remember Propp's definitions, but it is enlightening to read his list of these actions in the sequence in which they most often appear in the stories:

1. "absentation" (One of the members of a family absents himself from home.)

2. interdiction (An interdiction is addressed to the hero.)

3. violation (The interdiction is violated.)

4. reconnaissance (The villain makes an attempt at reconnaissance.)

5. delivery (The villain receives information about his victim.)

6. trickery (The villain attempts to deceive his victim.)

7. complicity (The victim submits to deception and thereby unwittingly helps his enemy.)

8. villainy (The villain causes harm or injury to a member of the family.)

9. mediation (The misfortune or lack becomes known.)

10. beginning counteraction (The seeker agrees to or decides upon a counter action.)

11. departure (The hero leaves home.)

12. the first function of the donor (The hero is tested, preparing the way for magical help.)

13. the hero's reaction (The hero reacts to the actions of the future donor.)

14. provision of a magical agent (The hero acquires the use of a magical agent.)

15. spatial transference between two kingdoms (The hero is led to the object of his search.)

⑯ struggle (The hero and the villain join in direct combat.)

⑰ branding, marking (The hero is branded.)

⑱ victory (The villain is defeated.)

⑲ removal of misfortune (The initial lack is liquidated.)

⑳ return (The hero returns.)

㉑ pursuit, chase (The hero is pursued.)

㉒ rescue (Rescue of the hero from pursuit.)

㉓ unrecognized arrival (The hero, unrecognized, arrives at home or in another country.)

㉔ unfounded claims (A false hero presents unfounded claims.)

㉕ difficult task (A difficult task is proposed to the hero.)

㉖ fulfillment (The task is fulfilled.)

㉗ recognition (The hero is recognized.)

㉘ exposure (The false hero or villain is exposed.)

㉙ transfiguration (The hero is given a new appearance.)

㉚ punishment (The villain is punished.)

㉛ wedding (The hero is married and ascends the throne.)

My simplified word definitions of Propp's actions

I simplified Propp's word definitions of the actions, and my amended list follows:

1. Adults leave or are absent from home because of work, business, or death.
2. Request or warning to the hero/ine.
3. Hero/ine disregards the warning and villain appears.
4. Villain asks question about the object or person he wants to get.
5. Villain gets the information.
6. Villain tricks the hero, assumes a disguise.
7. Hero/ine is fooled.
8. Villain steals the object or abducts a person.
8A. Someone in the family needs or desires to have something.
9. Hero/ine goes or is sent on journey to search for it and bring it back.
10. Hero/ine decides or agrees to go.
11. Hero/ine leaves home and meets a magical person, animal or witch.
12. Hero/ine is tested for kindness, sympathy, willingness to help.
13. Hero/ine reacts to the test.
14. Hero/ine is rewarded with magical thing/s.
15. Hero/ine is guided or directed to the object of his/her search.
16. Hero/ine confronts the villain by using cleverness or combat.
17. Hero/ine is wounded.
18. Villain is defeated.
19. The object of the search is obtained and the spell is broken.
20. Hero/ine escapes or returns.
21. Hero/ine is chased by the villain.
22. Hero/ine tries to save himself/herself by hiding; transforming, or placing obstacles.
23. Hero/ine arrives home unrecognized.
24. Someone else claims that he/she is hero/ine and claims the hero/ine's prize.

25) Hero/ine undertakes a test or task: ordeal, riddle guessing, choosing, or some other test.

26) Test or task is accomplished.

27) Hero/ine is finally recognized, appreciated.

28) Villain is exposed.

29) Hero/ine is given a new rank, appearance, or clothes.

30) Villain or impostor is punished.

31) Hero/ine is rewarded and is married.

If you think to yourself "Oh my, but there seem to be so many of these descriptions," just look at it in a different light: This is the entire set of building blocks from which all fairy tales are made! In any case, not all actions are present in each fairy tale. There are omissions, additions, jumps, and repetitions. Also, the tale may start with the second or the eleventh action, or any other. But, in general, the actions follow in chronological order and do not jump back and forward. Also, the tale may consist of several units, which Propp calls "moves," joined together. These moves could exist as separate stories on their own.

Although Propp's study was based on Russian fairy tales, it is now agreed that the analysis may be cross-culturally valid and more or less applicable to fairy tales from other parts of the world.

Propp theorized it might be possible to create an infinite number of new stories. And as you will see in numerous examples from my own research related in this book, his hypothesis was correct. In order to create a tale, one could take a sequence of the actions, drop some of them, repeat some, and supply the characters and settings. The sequence of Propp's actions would then become alive as tales.

Just like different melodies emanating from the twelve notes in the music scale, the actions in the sequence would give rise to different stories, while at the same time the stories would retain the basic elements. Of course, the process needs to be handled with great care, and attention has to be paid to all of the other elements in the tale—the connections, the motivations, and so on.

Propp says that storytellers receive material from their surroundings or from current realities and adapt them to the tale. In other words, the storytellers use symbolic imagery that is meaningful in the social and cultural context of their audience. That is why the use of Propp's system can be an invaluable tool for the creation of new stories, for anchoring and nourishing new growth from the tales' ancient roots.

Interestingly, there are parallels between Propp's and Jung's work, even though they worked within different fields. Both Propp and Jung focused on fairy tales. While Propp was concerned with the structure and the sequence of the tales, Jung was concerned with the structure and sequence of the psyche. Propp deals with actions and Jung with archetypes; both can be viewed as patterns of human behaviour. They both follow a certain path to achieve a goal. Basically, Propp's "sequence of actions" seems to describe the Jungian view of the "growth of the human psyche."

Exercising Creativity and Imagination

Gianni Rodari

Gianni Rodari was an Italian journalist and writer of children's books. He was awarded the Hans Christian Andersen Medal for children's literature, which gained him an international reputation as the best modern children's writer in Italian. Rodari was also a teacher who did extensive and innovative work with children in the classroom. His book *The Grammar of Fantasy* is the result of fifteen years of work in Italian schools. It is a manual for teachers, containing practical methods for guiding the imagination and for inventing stories.

Rodari's work with children and his innovative approach to teaching eventually became the core philosophy of the Reggio Emilia Schools in Italy. In this approach, both teacher and children engage in imaginative work and play together. The teacher does not pass on prepackaged knowledge for the children to memorize, but creates challenges for them, listens to children's responses, and then guides them in their projects. Then, the teacher actively participates and engages with the project along with the children. In this school environment, the children are not consumers of culture and values but become themselves the creators and producers of culture and values. Rodari understood that children need to play and use their imaginations, but that they need guidance from adults who listen to them.

Children must be encouraged and allowed to question, challenge, and recreate meaning through stories if they are to learn to think for themselves. This is especially important now, when children's lives are so prescribed and structured both at home and at school. Rodari regarded the fixed language in stories as detrimental to children's intellectual growth; he believed that all children should be entitled to use their creativity and imagination, not to become artists but so as not to be reduced to being copycats.

What is the imagination?

The imagination is sometimes defined as the act, or power, of forming mental images of what is not actually present, of what has never actually been experienced, or of creating new images or ideas by combining previous experiences. Imagination manifests itself particularly in the games of children. In a game, children combine facts they know from their experience with other information to construct a reality that corresponds to their needs and curiosity. Imagination propels us to think in new, unproven ways so that we reach solutions not thought of before. I should also add that, like many other human abilities, the imagination needs to be exercised or it will waste away. Like a muscle, it must be stretched or it will lose its tendency to be flexible.

In his work with children, Rodari used fairy tales as a starting point for games in which the children were challenged to invent their own stories. Rodari observed that young children are conservative in that they do not want their favourite fairy tales changed. They derive a sense of reassurance from recognizing the same words again and again. At a later stage, when they are ready to separate themselves from the tale, they are willing to accept the narrative as a parody. They dare to test their own personal boundaries by taking the tale apart and putting it back together in a different way, making it a game with a therapeutic effect. Examples of Rodari's games with fairy tales as described in his *The Grammar of Fantasy* can be found in Appendix B.

In Reggio Emilia Schools, Rodari and the teachers also experimented with Propp's system. They started by choosing twenty of Propp's actions, omitting some and substituting others. Then they produced twenty "playing cards," each marked with the title of one of Propp's actions, its definition, and a caricature drawing. The children mixed up the cards, drew a few at random, and made up a story, sometimes starting from the last card of the series. Because each card's action is open to many meanings and the structure of fairy tales resembles the structure of the child's experience, "the fairy tale's actions help children shed light on their own lives." [26]

Rodari's work is exemplary in its courage to confront the fixed texts of tales in a world where most people regard the print versions of the stories as something final and irrefutable. As a great advocate of children, Rodari gave them voice and the opportunity to express their own ideas within a school system.

In his work, Rodari focused on using the imagination. He wanted the children to experience the thrill of inventing and was not concerned with the tales themselves and their integrity. Consequently, the stories that children invented as a result of the classroom games seem more like improvisational fragments, stories that start going somewhere but get lost along the way. They do not come across as satisfying nor evoking deep emotions, as did their predecessors. Ideally, a game or a similar approach should enable children to create a tale using their own ideas and imagination and, at the same time, to create original, full, and emotionally satisfying stories.

How Children Respond to Stories

Arthur Applebee

Arthur Applebee is an educator, researcher, and author of numerous texts about teaching and language arts. In his book *The Child's Concept of Story,* a developmental study of children's storytelling and story comprehension skills, Applebee observes that there are at least three developmental stages in children's response to story. The stages are not just passed through, but they build upon each other like stepping stones and are integrated throughout the children's development.[27] In each of these stages, children respond to and learn from stories that interest them and fulfill their needs at their particular stage of development. Applebee describes the stages as follows:

① Preschool children

Preschool children aged 5 and under respond to realistic stories situated close to the home and its immediate surroundings. They like simple stories about the world they know and about animals and nature. In their response, they tend to focus on a single detail of the story and disregard the other aspects.

② Middle childhood

Between the ages of 6 and 10, children's interest shifts from realistic stories to stories set in distant and fantasy worlds. People and their actions dominate children's interest. Children of this age are interested in the offbeat and unusual, and they are much more likely to respond to such stories than to stories of everyday normal occurrences.

In this developmental period, fairy tales hold the children's greatest interest, particularly around the age of 8. The favourite narrative form at this stage involves a main character who goes through a series of adventures. They seem to view the plot of the story as a pattern of separate events. Before the age of 12, says Applebee, children show little ability to speculate and make predictions beyond the situation already described in the tale or to answer questions about the effects of the events on characters not so directly involved.

③ Adolescence

In adolescence, the children begin to recognize that the pattern of the story's events has a purpose. Once again their interests shift, this time from stories set in fantasy worlds to realistic ones. The children gradually develop the ability to analyze the events of the story, and they respond by generalizing about the story's meaning and by formulating statements about the story's theme or message.

To be able to generalize about the story's meaning, children have to pass through the stage where they could relate the story's experience to the situations with which they are familiar. Rarely, says Applebee, are students given a chance to make this sort of connection. Engagement with fairy tales by the method I describe in this book gives children the opportunity to make such a connection and thus prepares them for the next stage of the developmental response.

The children's preferences for certain types of stories in their particular developmental stages, according to Favat and Applebee, are strong and definite: When they want fairy tales, they do not want stories of reality; when they want realistic stories, they do not want fairy tales. If the books given to children aged between 7 and 9 do not provide the satisfaction the children are looking for, they may create obstacles for developing readers; children who seek stories set in fantasy worlds may avoid reading altogether.

Alternatively, where fairy tales are used for classroom activities with students in higher grades (such as grades 5 and 6), the benefits the stories could provide at an earlier stage of their development are not received because the intensity of the students' interest in fairy tales (therefore their receptiveness) is no longer there. The optimum time, then, to engage children with fairy tales is the period between ages 6 and 9.

My Work in the Classroom

Bruno Bettelheim points out that a fairy tale's enchantment depends to a considerable degree on the child's not quite knowing why he's delighted by it. Any discussion and explanation about what's going on takes away from the story's effect. To enhance that effect, it should be an interactive event shaped by those who participate in it.

The most effective way to present the tales in the classroom is with the participation of the children. This gives the children the opportunity to play inside the fairy-tale world and rehearse their emotional responses.

A Classroom Approach

An interactive storytelling and story-building session involves participation of the teacher/storyteller and the children/audience in an exercise of imagination, not one of literary analysis. Because children of grades 2 and 3 may not yet be able to express themselves well enough in written form, it is best to let them respond verbally first. The activities I do with the children are similar to the "emergent curriculum" in structure and can be viewed as a collaborative adventure shaped by both students and myself. [28]

The story-building activity that I use is student-driven, after I tell a sample fairy tale or story first. In that activity, I carefully listen to the children, respond to their answers, anticipate, and guide the children in the direction they want to go. The procedure in each classroom leaves room for surprises, allowing the students' work to take various paths. This interactive classroom procedure adheres to an important principle of the National Association for the Education of Young Children—children should be engaged in active rather than passive activities. Importantly, the activities should fit into the language curriculum within the listening and speaking (oral), reading and writing, and visual communications expectations for students in grades 2 and 3.

My classroom approach was tested with over 700 students in 23 classrooms in 15 schools, situated in different communities within the Greater Toronto Area and in Northern Ontario, including those of the Ojibway Nations. The demographics of these schools included children from diverse racial and socioeconomic backgrounds. Some schools were situated in low-income neighbourhoods and some in middle-class ones; students in one private school were from upper-middle class, high-income families. Some schools were in new suburban subdivisions and some in the inner city. There was great diversity among the inner-city schools as well: Some schools had large populations of recent immigrants, and many of the children did not yet speak English well; other schools had a very diverse ethnic and racial mix of students from all over the world and from a range of socioeconomic groups. In one inner-city school in a predominantly Chinese district, almost all students were of Chinese descent. In the schools on the First Nation reserve, located in bush and lake-filled territory, all the children were Ojibway. I also tested my approach in French immersion classes where the students tended to exhibit characteristics somewhat different from those in the regular classes.

Most of the student participants in my class-testing were children in grade 3. But I tested the approach in classroom sessions with students from grade 1 up to grade 8. These were often in classrooms with mixed grades.

Advantages of Symbols for Propp's Actions

Bettelheim noted that "unfed by our common fantasy heritage, the folk fairy tale, the child cannot invent stories on his own which help him cope with life's problems."[29] Following Propp's defined actions in the structure of the fairy tale, new tales can be generated, and the way children interpret them might mirror their own worlds. The tales help children by shedding light on their own lives, by providing the structure for their experiences. In the classroom, I find it helps to have a concrete tool to guide the re-creation of the story. So, my next step was the design and construction of a prototype teaching tool using Propp's sequence of actions to guide the children in their story creation and provide a scaffolding for their story. Recreating tales using Propp's actions allows the children to imbue them with meaning for themselves.

The multicultural demographics of schools in the city of Toronto, where the majority of my work took place, was a factor to be considered in creating the teaching tool and in the classroom approach. Many of the students speak limited English. To get across to them and make my proposed process for story creation understandable, it was essential to communicate Propp's actions through pictures and symbols.[30]

Graphic symbols can present complex facts in a simplified, more easily understood, more easily remembered form. They also get to the brain faster than the written word. Because symbols imply and suggest, one has freedom in interpreting them, which is what I wanted the children to have—the freedom to move and express themselves within the safety of the tale's structure.

The pictographs had to be in a game-like form so that the children could relate to them and remain attentive. After designing the pictographs, I copied them in black on neutral grey paper and attached them to magnetic vinyl sheets. Then I created maps of the journeys on which the stories' characters travelled, by assembling the pictographs in the linear sequence of events in the stories.

To create the map of the pictographs, I used two side-by-side portable magnetic boards to display the symbols of a story structure sequence. In addition to the magnetic pictographs, I placed magnetic buttons of various arbitrary sizes and colours to represent stories' characters. By doing so, I did not influence and thereby limit the children's visual imaginations. The button-characters were easy to move over the symbols, keeping everyone aware of where we were in the story's journey at any time during the classroom session.

The maps of the structures of fairy tales are the tools I used in the classroom sessions. The maps guided the children during the session's story creation, and the children remembered them and used them for inventing stories in the future.

Complete Set of Symbols

Pictographs representing Propp's actions

 1.   Parents leave or are absent from home

 2.   Request or warning to the hero/heroine

 3.   Hero/ine disregards the warning and villain appears

4.   Villain asks question about the object, person he wants to get

 5.   Villain gets the information

 6.   Villain tricks the hero, assumes a disguise

 7.   Hero/ine is fooled

 8.   Villain steals the object or abducts a person

 8a.   Parent needs or desires to have something

 9./10. Hero/ine goes or is sent on journey to search for it and bring it back

 11.   Hero/ine meets a magical animal or person

 12./13. Hero/ine is tested for kindness and help. Hero/ine reacts

14.   Hero/ine is rewarded by magical thing/s

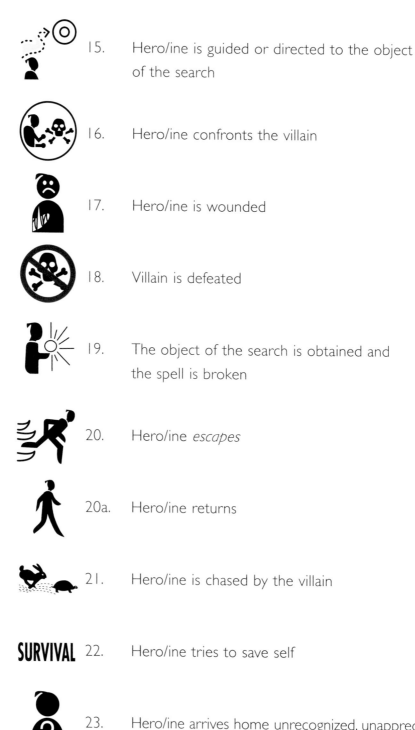

15. Hero/ine is guided or directed to the object of the search

16. Hero/ine confronts the villain

17. Hero/ine is wounded

18. Villain is defeated

19. The object of the search is obtained and the spell is broken

20. Hero/ine *escapes*

20a. Hero/ine returns

21. Hero/ine is chased by the villain

SURVIVAL 22. Hero/ine tries to save self

23. Hero/ine arrives home unrecognized, unappreciated

24. Someone else claims to be the hero/ine and claims the prize

 25./26. Hero/ine undertakes test or task. Test or task is accomplished

 27. Hero/ine is recognized

 28. Villain is exposed

 30. Villain or impostor is punished

 30a. Villain or impostor is punished

 31. Hero/ine is rewarded and/or is married

Additional symbols

 1a. Home (additional symbol for ending of story)

 x. dispatching ritual (another additional symbol)

In three instances (actions 9 and 10, 12 and 13, and 25 and 26), I have combined two of Propp's actions and represented them as one symbol because the second action is implied in the first. For Propp's actions 20 and 30, I have provided a choice of two graphics so the more suitable one could be used, depending upon the story.

Sample action-symbol maps

The maps of the journeys, as they were used in the session:

Tale Type: The Children and the Ogre

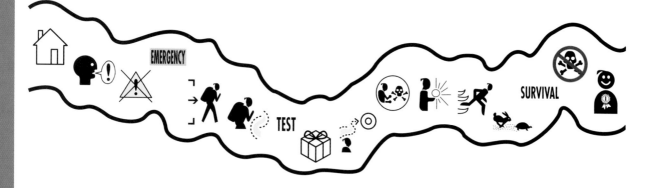

Tale Type: The Animal Bride

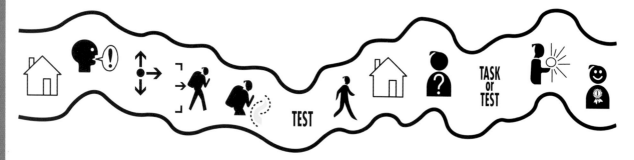

Tale Type: Magic Objects

The Classroom Procedure

Each school session lasted about an hour and, in most cases, was followed by an unstructured period such as recess or lunch or dismissal so that impressions from the session could be reflected upon rather than being diluted by other structured activities. The session took place either in the classroom or in the library. Usually the children sat on the floor around me, or they remained at their desks. Their location did not seem to make any difference to the results.

1. I started the session by telling one of the tales to the children. I did not use any illustrated material during reading because I did not want to influence the children's own imagination or set any visual precedent for the children's follow-up creation of their own story.

2. Then, using my magnetic board with the magnetic-button-characters, I told the students only that the sketch showed the road on which the characters travelled. Briefly, I recounted the tale once again while at the same time moving the magnetic button-characters over the pictographic symbols to demonstrate the hero/ine's journey.

3. Next, I suggested that, together, we could invent a similar story. By posing non-leading questions, I guided the children and elicited

their ideas and snippets of dialogue for the new story's characters, asking about who they would choose as the main character: "Who is it going to be? What will be the character's name?" And so on. After each question, children would raise their hands to respond. I would point to a student, listen to the suggestion, and usually take it. The first ideas were often the best because they were spontaneous reactions to what went on in the story they had listened to. Sometimes, I allowed a few students to express their ideas, then chose the one that seemed fresh and unlike any previous suggestions. However, I acknowledged all the ideas by commenting that they were good and could work equally well in our story, which was true.

④ After I picked a student's suggestion, I would elicit approval from the class. If some children objected, we would vote to decide which route to take. If one student tried to monopolize the input of suggestions, I would purposefully allow other students to express their ideas and thereby encourage participation to ensure that the story was not moulded by a single student.

⑤ I placed no restrictions on the children's ideas, giving them absolute freedom to invent. After taking a suggestion, I would tie it into the story with a sentence, then ask "And what happens next?" A student would answer, "Max panics," to which I would respond, "What does he do?" and so on until the class story unfolded.

⑥ The children were the ones in control of the story and my function, as their guide, was to listen to their ideas and weave them into the story. At all times, the children could see the story map and the action symbols as I moved the button-characters: Everyone could see where we were in the story.

⑦ After we had created the story, I summarized it while simultaneously replaying it on the story map with the magnetic button-characters, and I would ask the children to correct any mistakes.

⑧ As a last step in the classroom session, I asked the children to draw the scene that they found the most interesting from our newly created story. I suggested that they try to visualize the story as a movie and draw the scene from their imaginations. I allowed approximately fifteen minutes for this activity and encouraged the children to put lots of detail into their work.

⑨ This drawing segment of the classroom procedure is important and allows the children to each create their personal expression of the story's meaning. When the children finished their drawings, I collected them. Some of their drawings are reproduced with my commentary in Chapter 5 of this book.

⑩ Before leaving the school, I asked the teacher to wait three weeks, then ask the students to write their recollection of the story I told them and the story they had created. When I returned on my second classroom visit, I repeated the same procedure, but read a different story.

Expressing Response through Drawing

The children's drawings were a significant component of my research study and just as important as the children's verbal creation of the story. Although the class-created story was a collaborative effort, the drawings allowed more individual expression and individual retelling of the story. In other words, each child had a further opportunity to make the story his or her own, to personalize it, to add to or embellish it.

Most children of this age do not have confidence in their writing skills or they are struggling, which can obviously be a deterrent to the clear and truthful expression of their ideas. Howard Gardner, the author of *Artful Scribbles, The Significance of Children's Drawings*, says that, "until the task of writing has been mastered, the system of drawing is the only one sufficiently elaborated to permit expression of inner life." However, this particular phenomenon lasts only briefly, as suggested by Rose Alschuler and LaBerta Hattwick, authors of the massive study *Painting and Personality*:

> By the time the children are nine or ten years of age, they have, as a rule, been so thoroughly infused with the need for reproducing exactly what they see that their own natural modes of self-expression have been blocked off and the earlier impulses to paint and express themselves from within have very largely been stifled. [31]

When it came to my analysis of the children's drawings, I determined that there would be no evaluation of the children's drawing skills and no response to the prettiness, decorativeness, or vibrant colours of the drawings, unless the colour was used to express meaning. The content of the drawings was my sole concern.

Selecting stories

For my work in the classroom, I purposely stayed away from well-known fairy tales. Young children often don't want their favourite story changed because they derive a sense of reassurance from the sameness. Since my time in the classroom was limited to one hour, I did not want to face this obstacle. When choosing the stories for my project, I asked myself whether they fit the following criteria:

1. Potential appeal to children; partly based upon whether and how the tale deals with problems that the children themselves experience or can relate to, such as low self-esteem, fear of abandonment, struggle for independence, self-reliance, bullying, and envy
2. Simple, straightforward plot
3. Presence of magic
4. Potential for interactive play and replacement of the story's symbolic elements

At the end of this book, I have included an anthology of tales, ready for use in the classroom. If you would like to work with other tales, use my description of the procedure in Appendix B. But be prepared: Searching for stories in their different global guises, comparing them in order to gain understanding and then uncovering the stories' structures through Propp's analysis is a time-consuming task.

Tale Type: The Children and the Ogre

Surprisingly, a small child protagonist is rather rare in fairy tales. But in this popular and important tale type, there is a child standing alone against the ogres of the adult world, a hero or heroine with whom children can readily identify. These stories deal with a number of issues that concern children—fear of abandonment, self-reliance, and struggle for independence. The child protagonist has to be compassionate, resourceful, and cunning, not only to succeed but simply to survive. Importantly, the child must act upon his own initiative. In this tale type, I found stories containing four different plot structures. For classroom use, I chose a story rooted in Russian folklore called "The Black Geese of Baba Yaga."

This story appealed to me because it has a straightforward plot and only one heroine. Many other tales of this type have two or more child protagonists, as if to strengthen the image of a child. The story also has the motif of the "obstacle flight," the escape by means of a magic object, an element that promises to be especially appealing. Alison Lurie's retelling of this story in her book *Clever Gretchen and Other Forgotten Folktales* became the base that I further adapted and shortened. For instance, instead of using her three repetitions of the same event (in this case a meeting with a magic animal), I used only one encounter in order to conserve class time for the children's creation of their own tale. The following is my version of the story as adapted for and told in a grade 3 class.

The story: "The Black Geese of Baba Yaga"

Once there was a man and a woman who had two children, a girl and a boy. One day the parents had to go to the market so the mother said to her daughter, "Elena, while we're away, take care of your baby brother. But be careful! The black geese of Baba Yaga were seen flying over the village. So don't go outside. When we come back we'll bring you some sugar buns."

Elena knew about Baba Yaga. She was the terrible witch of the forest, who was eight feet tall and ate little children. After her parents left, Elena stayed in the house with her brother, but after a while she got bored. She saw her friends outside, so she took her brother, set him out on the grass, and went to play with her friends, forgetting all about him.

After some time, she remembered and came back to look for him. But he was nowhere to be found. Then, far on the horizon, Elena saw the black geese. They were carrying something! She realized what must have happened: The black geese had taken her brother and were carrying him to Baba Yaga's hut. "I must go after him," she decided and she ran toward the forest where Baba Yaga lived.

As she went over the fields, she came to a pond. There, lying on the sand was a fish, gasping. "Elena," the fish called. "Please help me. I'm dying!" Now, Elena was in a hurry, but she stopped and put the fish back into the water. The fish popped her head out and said, "Because you helped me, I will help you. Pick up that shell which lies by your feet. If you're ever in danger, throw the shell over your shoulder and it will help you."

Elena couldn't see how the shell could possibly help her, but she didn't want to seem rude. So she picked up the shell and put it in her pocket. Then she ran on into the dark forest where trees grew so close together that not even a ray of light could shine through. Finally she came to a clearing, and there was Baba Yaga's hut. It stood on two giant chicken feet, and the black geese were sleeping on its roof. Elena crawled to the hut and peeked inside. There was water boiling on the stove, but Baba Yaga was lying down, snoring.

Elena's brother was near her, sitting on the ground, playing with some bones. Elena crept in, grabbed her baby brother, and ran outside. But the black geese saw her. They honked and flapped their wings. It woke up Baba Yaga. She ran out and screamed, "Stop thief! Bring back my dinner!" And she ran after them.

Elena ran as fast as she could, but she was carrying her brother and he was heavy. Baba Yaga was getting closer and closer. When Elena looked back, she saw Baba Yaga within an arm's length. What could she do?

She remembered about the shell and she threw it over her shoulder. Instantly a big wide river appeared behind her. Baba Yaga could not go around it, so she waded into it. But the water was deep and Baba Yaga couldn't swim.

It didn't take long before she drowned. Elena got home with her brother just in time, as their parents returned and brought them some sugar buns.

The actions in the story

"The Black Geese of Baba Yaga"

Here is the sequence of Propp's actions as they appear in this story, with my symbols that represent them.

 1. Parents leave or are absent from home

 2. Request or warning to the hero/ine

 3. Hero/ine disregards the warning and villain appears

 8. Villain steals the object or abducts a person

 9./10. Hero/ine goes or is sent on journey to search for it and bring it back

 11. Hero/ine meets a magical animal or person

 12./13. Hero/ine is tested for kindness and help and reacts

14. Hero/ine is rewarded by magical thing/s

 15. Hero/ine is guided or directed to the object of the search

 16. Hero/ine confronts the villain

 19. The object of the search is obtained and the spell is broken

 20. Hero/ine escapes

 21. Hero/ine is chased by the villain

SURVIVAL 22. Hero/ine tries to save him/herself

 30. Villain or impostor is punished

31. Hero/ine is rewarded and/or is married

Note: Breaks occur in the number sequence of Propp's actions because I have listed only the actions that take place in this story.

Action-symbol map of "The Black Geese of Baba Yaga"

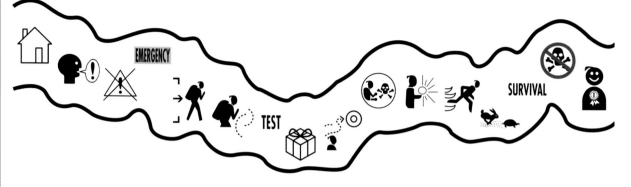

Creating a new story

This session took place in a First Nation school on a reserve in Northern Ontario. All the children were Ojibway students in grade 3.

My questions and students' answers

My lead question: Who should be the hero/ine? Is it a boy or a girl?

Students' answer: A boy!

Ⓠ What will be his name?

Ⓐ *Matthew*

Ⓠ Does Matthew have a brother or a sister?

Ⓐ *Sister, Mia*

Ⓠ Who else is at home? Who is in charge?

Ⓐ *Mother and father*

Ⓠ The parents are going somewhere. Where are they going?

Ⓐ *To play bingo*

Ⓠ What kind of responsibility do they give to Matthew? (For instance: to look after some object, or someone, like a sibling or pet)

Ⓐ *Watch your sister.*

Q What warning do the adults give to the hero? Is there someone dangerous?

A *Bobcat, cougar*

Q What happens after the adults leave?

A *Matthew and baby sister Mia are inside of the house, watching TV. Cougar jumps in through the window, picks up baby Mia and carries her outside into a bush.*

Q What does Matthew do?

A *He panics. He goes to look for Mia.*

Q Whom does Matthew meet? (The best is a magic animal, but it could be magical person or a talking object)

A *A purple squirrel*

Q The squirrel is in some trouble. What is happening to her?

A *She is choking.*

Q What does Matthew do to help the squirrel?

A *He squeezes her stomach.* (The student stands up and demonstrates the Heimlich manoeuvre.)

Q What does the squirrel do after that? How does she respond?

A *She gives Matthew a magic stone.*

Q What happens next?

A *Matthew sees a cave. He goes inside.*

Q What does the cave look like inside? Describe it.

A *It is mouldy there, and there are spider webs.*

Q Is the cougar there?

A *No, he isn't, but baby Mia is there.*

Q What is she doing?

A *She is crying.*

Q Then what happens?

A Matthew takes Mia and runs. Cougar is chasing after them.

Q What does Matthew do?

A He throws the magic stone over his shoulder.

Q What happens?

A It hits the cougar and changes him into a frog!

Q Then what?

A Matthew goes home with Mia. Parents return home from bingo and bring money and chips.

At this point, I summarize the class-created story and ask them to correct me in case I make any mistakes. At the same time, I move the magnetic button-characters across the trail on the action-symbol map to show the class how the characters advance throughout the story. The story as invented by the grade 3 students at the First Nation school on the Ojibway Reserve follows:

Story from a First Nation school: "Cougar"

Matthew has a sister called Mia. His parents are going to play bingo. Before they leave, they say to Matthew, "Be careful. We saw a cougar nearby." Matthew and Mia stay inside of the house and watch TV. In jumps the cougar, breaks through a window; snatches baby Mia; and carries her outside into the bush.

Matthew panics. He goes to look for her. In the bush he meets a magic purple squirrel. She's choking; Matthew squeezes her stomach to help her. To thank him, the squirrel gives Matthew a magic stone.

Matthew sees a cave. He goes inside. It is mouldy there

and there are spider webs. Mia is inside alone and she's crying. Matthew takes Mia and runs. The cougar sees them and chases after them. Matthew throws the magic stone over his shoulder. The stone hits the cougar and changes him into a frog. Matthew and Mia get home. When their parents return from bingo, they bring money and chips.

For comparison, the following children's story was created by children from a grade 3 French immersion class from a public school in Toronto. It was created using the same action-symbol map and same line of questioning.

Story from a public school: "Baker"

Lily lives with her grandparents. One day, her grandfather goes fishing and her grandmother goes shopping for knitting yarn. They say to Lily, "Watch grandmother's jewels while we're away. Inside of the jewels, there is grandmother's secret recipe."

Lily goes outside and climbs a tree in the garden but gets stuck in the branches. When she finally gets down and goes back into the house, she discovers that grandma's jewels were stolen. The evil baker stole the jewels for the secret recipe, so that he could become the most famous baker in the world.

Lily goes to find the jewels so she can bring them home. She meets a dragon whose wing is broken. Lily takes some leaves and wraps the dragon's wing with them. The dragon says, "Thank you for your help. Here, take my golden egg. If you are in danger, put the egg on the ground and the first person to pass by it will fall asleep for a long, long time."

Lily continues on her journey and smells the scent of her grandma's cookies. She follows the smell. She comes to a hut made out of buns and bread. There is nobody inside as the baker went to wash his pots in the river.

Lily goes inside of the baker's house and gets her grandmother's jewels and takes some of the cookies there as well, and runs. There is a guard dog that barks when it sees her. The baker hears him and runs after Lily. Lily puts the dragon's egg on the ground, and when the baker passes by it, he falls down and goes to sleep.

Lily gets back and when her grandparents return, they say to her, "Thank you." Her grandma suggests that they bake some of her cookies, but Lily does not feel like it because she ate all of the cookies that she took from the baker's house and is full.

Discussion of Results

The focus of my original research was to find out whether children could liberate the folktale they heard from its fixed narrative and make it their own. The results of the study showed that they can do so very easily when provided with permission, opportunity, and guidance. In all sessions, original and different stories were created in the classroom. The stories reflected the children's personal lives, the places they lived in, and the knowledge they have accumulated about the world.

Identification with the hero/ine

Perhaps because the children hear the sample story first and therefore know that the protagonist comes out victorious in the end, they seem to identify easily with the hero/ine of the story they create together, as demonstrated in several ways:

① In most of the sessions, the children name the hero/ine of the story after themselves or one of their classmates or friends or someone in their families.

② Many children of colour portray the hero/ine of the story as a person of colour in their drawings, suggesting that they see themselves or someone like them as the main character.

③ Some male students identify with female protagonists. For instance, a boy suggested that the girl-heroine of the story climb a tree. When questioned afterwards as to why he made that suggestion, he said that is what he likes to do. Bruno Bettelheim noted that a child cannot cast himself in the role of a figure of the other sex on the first hearing of a fairy tale because it takes distance and personal elaboration over time. But in the "re-creation" of a tale, we are already one step ahead of just hearing it. When children actively participate in a tale, the identification seems to happen much sooner.

④ In some of the written recollections of their stories, children switch halfway through their writing from third- to first-person narration.

The children seem to want the story to be about them. That corresponds with the self-centred view of the world that children hold at this particular stage of their development.

Making meaning by personalizing the stories

The children bring images that reflect the places they live in and their lifestyle into the stories they create in the classroom.

Example 1

In the First Nation school on the Ojibway reserve in Northern Ontario, the parents in the class story go to play bingo. While the hero watches TV with his little sister at home, a cougar breaks in through the window and takes the girl.

Figure 1 (from "Cougar" story)

In the picture there is a bingo hall on the right and cars arriving with headlights on, indicating the evening. In the house on the left side of the illustration, a broken windowpane is visible. Beside the house there is the cougar, carrying the child away.

 After the session, the teacher commented that the parents going to play bingo is a fact of life on the reserve. Also, the children mentioned that a cougar was recently spotted in the area, so it was quite a real and present danger for them.

Example 2

In midtown Toronto in a private school whose students come from high-income families, the heroine of the story is at home with her big brother. He goes to a sporting event and tells the heroine to look after a precious china teacup. She makes hot chocolate in that cup and drinks it by the fireplace. The wizard, who is like Santa Claus, comes through the chimney and steals the china teacup.

Figure 2 (from "Wizard" story)

In the Wizard's house there is an electronic gate, a surveillance camera, the Wizard's safe, and teapots placed on an alarm system. This suggestion may be inspired by the home security systems the children have in their own homes. The heroine in the picture is wearing designer-brand clothes (Abercrombie) while thinking about her brother at the boxing match. Note the thought balloon in the illustration in Figure 2.

Example 3

Figure 3 (from "Wizard" story)

The Wizard's house consists of many rooms, perhaps a reflection of these students' homes. There are rooms dedicated to specific purposes such as the "planing room" with TV screens; the "fire room" with a fireplace; the "drinking room"; the "bedroom"; "THE room"; the "TV room" in which we see a character with a remote control; the "Potion Room"; and the "Storage Room" for money. There is also an evil housekeeper on the right, and there are several protective lasers on the roof. These two examples of stories, one from a First Nation school and the other one from a private school, show clearly the effect of the children's lifestyles on the stories they create.

Reflection of children's homes and families

The diversity of family background is seen in the children's stories. The families vary from two mothers living together to a single-father family. Often, there are older siblings or babysitters at home with the story's protagonist.

Example 4

In one story created by a public school class, we had both a mother and a stepmother at home.

Figure 4

In the picture, the two mothers are returning from the shopping mall, bringing the hero a pet bat as a present. The children in the classroom took the family situation consisting of two mothers for granted. When I appeared confused, the initiating child proceeded with an explanation—that the parents got divorced and the father was remarried and then he died. The two mothers moved in together.

After the session I questioned the teacher about it. I was told that the year previously there was a case of a family in that situation. It was implied that the child's suggestion might have been her own experience. The real surprise for me was the public display of matter-of-fact acceptance of parental death by classmates. Given the school's demographics, particularly its large recent-immigrant population, however, it may not be so surprising. Many of these children experienced the harshness of life before they came to Canada.

Interestingly, in none of the stories is there a sole-mother staying home with the child hero. This seems to indicate that the mother is probably working. The families that children portray in their stories mirror today's norm.

Modern world, contemporary objects

Children place the stories they create in the contemporary world, even though they know they are inventing a fairy tale. They place pieces of modern furniture, appliances, TV sets, playgrounds, and highway signs in their drawings, which show that they put themselves and the world they live in into the fairy tales.

Example 1

Figure 5

The drawing (Figure 5) portrays the inside of the hero's house with a refrigerator, a TV set, a remote control, and a sofa—obviously objects of contemporary living.

Example 2

Figure 6

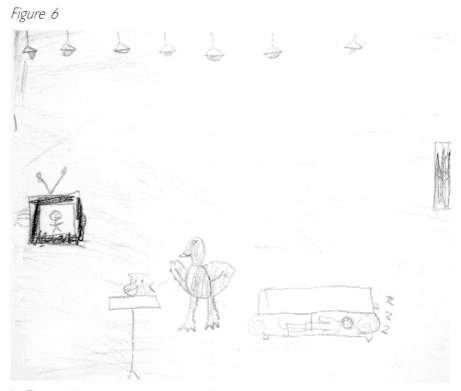

In Figure 6, you can see a track lighting system in the living room along with a TV set and a sofa.

Example 3

Figure 7

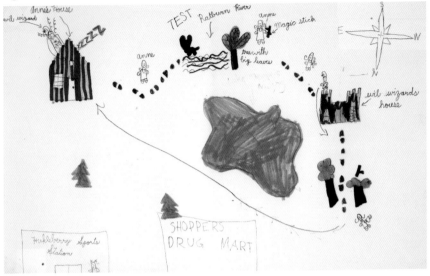

This student included "Shoppers Drug Mart" as a part of the story's landscape, indicating her world and contemporary life.

Solving the hero's problem
by applying existing knowledge

Because the stories provide the children with the opportunity for problem solving, children reach into their own knowledge resources and creatively apply that knowledge to the actions of the story's protagonist. They come to test themselves in the safety of the story's situation and they resolve the hero's problems.

In one story I tell the class, the heroine encounters a fish lying on the sand by the pond, gasping for air. The fish calls, "Help me! I'm dying!" The solution to the heroine's test is simple because it is obvious. She puts the fish back into the water.

In the stories the children create in the class, the tests are far more complex and require ingenious solutions and resourcefulness from the children. They have to rely on the personal knowledge they have acquired to this point in their lives.

Example 1

In the First Nation school, the hero of the story meets a purple squirrel that is choking.[32] The hero helps the choking squirrel by performing the Heimlich manoeuvre. During our classroom session, this move was demonstrated by the child who had made the suggestion.

Example 2

In one inner-city public school, the hero meets a genie who is stuck in quicksand (see Figure 8). The student who suggested that the hero use a rope to pull the genie out showed awareness of the situation and must have had knowledge of the properties of quicksand. Using the rope, but from a distance, the hero can safely rescue the genie.

Figure 8

When the children create a test for the hero of the story they create, they also have to resolve the hero's dilemma to ensure his survival. To do that, they have to step into their hero's shoes in order to identify with him; then they reach into their own stored knowledge to resolve the dilemma. In other words, the children come full circle to test themselves.

Villains

If the hero of the story embodies reality, the villain embodies the supernatural and its malevolent, life-threatening aspect. At the Ojibway First Nation schools, the children's choice of villain for their stories related directly to the place in which they lived. In one instance the cougar-villain is quite realistic, probably because a cougar had recently been spotted in their vicinity. In another instance, the Sasquatch-villain is a part of Aboriginal lore.

In Toronto schools, the children suggested a stereotypical villain for their story. In the classroom stories, we had the vampire Dracula, a dragon, a werewolf, witches, and wizards. However, the children would add unique features to these stereotypical villains, making them their own personalized creations.

Examples

Figure 9 ABC

In one story, Dracula reads a book (Figure 9A). In another, the wizard enters dwellings through the chimney like Santa Claus (Figure 9B). Still another has a dragon who is a father, living with his baby dragon-son (Figure 9C).

In addition to the existing villain-stereotypes, a new breed of villains emerged from the pop culture as the children's other suggestions included Frankenstein, Dr. Octopus (from "Spiderman"), and the Green Goblin. Sometimes evil characters from video games were suggested as the villain of the class-created stories.

Ultimately, the choice of villain for the class-created story rested on me because I either took or discarded the children's suggestions—with class approval, of course. When children suggested a stranger, a big fat ugly man, or a kidnapper as villains, I did not accept those suggestions because I felt uneasy with them. I was a visitor in the classroom and did not know the children personally, so I was not prepared to deal with any overtly realistic situation and where that situation might lead. My responsibility as an adult in the classroom was to exercise moral and ethical judgment to protect the rest of the children. In my school sessions, I preferred a fantasy figure as villain for the class-created tale.

Making magic

Expressing their own view of the world

Sometimes at the beginning of a class session, I would ask the children what they liked best about fairy tales. The answers were unanimous—"The magic," they said. Because the magic is important to children, I would like to show you the visuals of how some children handled the segment of the story where magic comes into play, and discuss the reactions.

In "The Black Geese of Baba Yaga" that I read to the class, the fish gives Elena a shell which, after being thrown over the shoulder, creates a wide river. In some class sessions, the students created the magic in a similar way:

Example 1

In one story, the mole gives the heroine a magic tree branch which, when tapped three times on the ground, makes thorny bushes grow. The pursuing wizard becomes impaled on the thorns (Figure 10 and Figure 11). In the second picture (Figure 11), the student tries to soften the goriness of it by adding butterflies and a ladybug.

Figure 10 (from "Wizard" story)

Figure 11 (from "Wizard" story)

In many classroom sessions, the magic that the students injected into their class-created story was not modelled on the form of magic in "The Black Geese of Baba Yaga" tale. They felt free to invent their own form of magic while keeping the ultimate goal in mind ... to stop the villain and get the hero home safely.

Example 2

In another class-created story, a purple squirrel gives a rock to the hero. When the rock is thrown at the villain (the cougar), it causes the cougar to transform into a frog. Instead of creating an obstacle in the path of the pursuing villain, their thrown rock renders the villain harmless by transforming him into a frog (Figure 12 and Figure 13).

Figure 12 ("Cougar" story)

In this child's drawing, we see the cougar at the moment of transformation into a frog.

Figure 13 (from "Cougar" story)

This child's illustration (Figure 13) shows the completion of the cougar's transformation into a frog. This student visualized the scene taking place inside the cave, while the previous student illustrated it happening outside. Transformation is difficult to portray, yet several students chose just this moment and successfully captured it.

Example 3

In "Birdman," another of the children's stories, a tree tells the heroine to find the magic pebble. The pebble becomes the key to enter and exit the magic realm.

Figure 14 (from "Birdman" story)

In the child's drawing, the heroine is at the entrance to another world, standing at the edge of a cliff, by a tree that talks. Note the speech balloon coming from the tree, as if it is giving instructions to the heroine about what to do next and how to gain entry to the magic realm.

Figure 15 (from "Birdman" story)

Figure 15 shows the heroine exiting the magic realm and passing by the talking tree. This student artist added springs to the heroine's running shoes to help her run faster or, perhaps, to show us how fast she runs. His interpretation of the villain, the birdman in the story, shows the fusion of a human with a bird. The rooster-like crown on the birdman's head and his gigantic beak indicate his power and strength. The tree's facial expression is intense, as if to scare off the birdman and help the heroine escape. In the speech balloon are the villain's thoughts: "What is that tree doing their [*sic*]?"

Figure 16 (from "Birdman" story)

Another student's interpretation of the same scene shows the birdman getting embedded in the tree, which acts as a portal between the two worlds. In the speech balloon, the birdman comments on his predicament, "How did that happin [*sic*]? Oh ya, that magic pepel [*sic*]. Rats."

When the adult gets lost

In one of the sessions, an unexpected situation emerged during our story-creating process. In the children's story, the cat gives the hero a coin worth three small wishes, and the hero uses all three wishes to find and free his lost dog. As a result, when the witch was in pursuit of him, there was no magic wish left to help the hero escape. At that moment, I felt at a loss, not knowing how to bring the hero back home safely. So I asked the children. Spontaneously using their ingenuity, the children solved the problem and saved the hero by explaining "Mondays are bad days for witches." So they had the witch cast her spell to stop the hero but, because it was Monday, the spell did not work!

Figure 17 ("Witch" story)

In the student's picture (Figure 17), the witch stands near her stove, casting a spell that does not work. The calendar can be seen, indicating "Monday, bad day." The student added other scary objects such as a spider, a spider web, and ghosts hanging from the ceiling. The hero and his dog are on the run, and the hero still holds on to the magic coin even though it is now worthless.

Inventing magic was incredibly easy for the children because, at this particular stage of their development, they view the world as one where both the real and the fantastic are accepted on the same plane of human experience. The story-creating activity provides children with the opportunity to express the way they see the world at their age. Their interest in the "magical" is further affirmed by the majority of the children who choose to portray the scene of the story set in the "magic realm" in their drawings.

The way children spontaneously handle the "logic" in the magic they create is consistent with the internal logic governing the magic in fairy tales, where the magic object creates something conforming to its natural ability. For example, a pebble makes a mountain, a branch creates thorny bushes, a coin buys wishes. In other words, children create the magical incidents in the stories in a true folktale manner.

Back to the real world

In the sample story, the parents return home from the market and bring the heroine a gift of sugar buns, which they had promised her before they left. In the class sessions, we did not establish at the beginning of our stories what the adults would bring when they came back. Yet the children made spontaneous, logical connections between the gift and the place the adults went to at the story's opening; for example:

1. Parents bring money and chips from a Bingo game.

2. Big brother brings boxing gloves from the sports event.

3. Parents bring pizza from the market in the mall.

4. Parents bring a slice of cake from the party.

On a few occasions, the children made an implied joke about the gift in their story. In Figure 4, the two mothers return from the shopping mall and bring a pet bat as a gift for the hero. The hero does not like the gift because it reminds him of his experience with a vampire bat and makes him think that it could happen again.

A similar joke shows up in another story in which the parents, on the way home from dinner, stumble upon the villain's skull and bring it home as a keepsake for the hero because they know he likes scary stuff.

In the story about an evil baker, the grandmother wants to bake cookies, but the heroine is already full of the cookies she gorged on at the evil baker's house. Instinctively, the children understood that a story is more satisfying when they inject a little joke as comic relief from the tension.

Video games are sometimes compared to spatial storytelling. In magazines for "gamers," editors produce maps when explaining the experience of game playing. The influence of video games on the children's class-created stories can be seen in the drawings that portray the story in the form of a map.

Figure 18

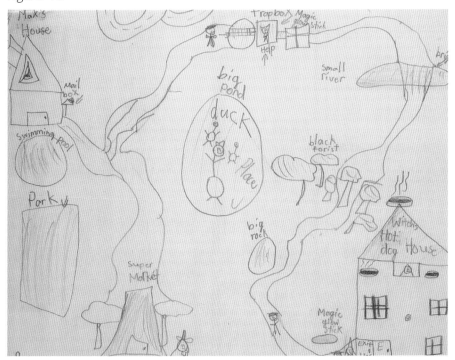

In Figure 18, the student created a complex map of the story, personalized by adding things that were not in the class-created tale, such as a swimming pool, a park, and a supermarket. We start to travel in the top left corner of the map in a game-like progression, having to cross the bridge and free a rabbit from a trap box in order to receive a magic glow stick instead of a carrot, as in the class story. Another bridge has to be crossed, and then we enter the black forest, bypass a big rock to finally arrive at the "Witch's Hot dog House." We exit at the bottom right corner through the door marked "Exit way."

Figure 19

The map in Figure 19 is showing the way home from the castle. The hero and his sister have to get past the alligators, an element added by the student, and through the circle of danger to get to a tree-lined path leading back to the hero's house.

Figure 20

The student has illustrated the hero in progression as he is climbing down under the river to get to the treasure chest in the upper right corner. There is an exit sign on the bottom right.

When looking at the children's maps, I am reminded of the games of my childhood in Prague when we children created mazes on the sidewalks with chalk. We then pushed and navigated shards of broken glass across the lines and spaces of the maze. The striking difference between the mazes of my childhood and the maps the children drew in their pictures is that we progressed in movement from left to right, influenced no doubt by reading text in books. But the maps the children have drawn show circular movement, as in Figure 18, or vertical movement, as in Figures 19 and 20; such graphic devices are likely the result of playing video games.

Video and computer games are a reality of today's generation, a fact that educators have to accept. Rather than consider playing video games in a negative light, consider that the games provide the children with a vast reservoir of images. Never before have children had access to such a large store of visual vocabulary. The fact that the children used imagery from computer and video games in their class-created stories suggests that their play with computer and video games is not just passive receivership of the designer's created universe. The children can harvest the games' elements and imagery to use like building blocks for creating something new.

Some children did that in our classroom sessions. There could not be a better example of this than the story created by a child with autism. Upon my arrival at the suburban school, the teacher told me that a boy with autism was a member of the class, and that the boy never participated and he did not draw or write. I was told not to be surprised by his lack of response. Before I show you the boy's story, let me tell you the story that his class created.

"Witch" story

Max lives with his dad and his dog, called Blue. One day, the father goes to his friend's house and says to Max, "Don't go outside with your dog because there is a witch around here who steals pets."

When his father leaves, Max goes to a store with the dog. When he comes out of the store, his dog is missing. Max goes to find Blue. As he walks through the streets, he meets a magic cat. The cat says to Max, "I am very hungry. Can you give me some food?" Max goes back home to get some food for the cat. He brings it back for the cat to eat. The cat is grateful. The cat says, "Since you helped me, I will help you." She gives Max a magical coin that guarantees him three small wishes.

Max's first wish is to find out where his dog Blue is. His second wish is to get to that place. When he gets there, he sees a scary house. Outside, there are cages with many different pets. There are hamsters, turtles, and other dogs. Max finds his dog Blue and uses his third remaining wish to get him out of the cage. Then he runs home with Blue.

Meanwhile, the witch is in the house cooking and not suspecting anything. She looks out and sees that her new pet is missing. She chases after Max and Blue and casts a spell on them to stop them. But her spell does not work because it happened to be a bad day for witches' magic. So Max and Blue got home safely.

When the father comes back home, he brings ice cream for Max and his dog.

The children started to work on their drawings and the teacher noticed that the boy she had identified was writing something, which seemed to her to be highly unusual. Three times the boy came to us and asked us how to spell such words as "throw" and "sword," and I wondered why he needed to know these since they were not in our story. The child continued to write throughout recess while the others went outside to play. At the start of a new class period, the child handed me his paper. This is what he had written:

> The dad say don't go out side with your dog but then Zelda dad go out Zelda don't know what his dad say so he take his dog and he forgot to look at his dog so he look and his dog was missing so he ran he saw the magic whale he lift him and throw the magic whale and the magic whale give Zelda a magic coin it grab 3 wish fist he wish he got a map he get in the cave he saw a which making a soup now he see his dog and a chest Zelda open the inside the chest was a big heart now he got 4 life he wish his dog was free and it did and Zelda run away but the wich was chasing him and Zelda wish he got a master sword the most powerful sword in the earth but the wich made Zelda have 1 life and Zelda deafet the wich and Zelda and his dog was home even his dad give Zelda a present and Zelda open and it was a boomerang Zelda like the boomerang his dad was happy.

The story was astonishing, but there were parts that were unrecognizable. Things were added to the story that appeared to be from video games. The protagonist's name is "Zelda" not "Max" as it was in the class story. There is a magic whale that gives the magic coin instead of a cat, as in the story. The whale might be a reference to the fish from the sample story. The fish was thrown back into the water by the heroine. There is a cave instead of a house where the witch is cooking her soup. But there is also a chest with a big heart inside and four lives, like in the "Zelda" video game. The story really becomes the boy's story when Zelda gets the master sword, confronts the witch, defeats her, and then gets the boomerang present from his father.

What this student with autism did is exactly what I was hoping to see. He created his very own story, integrating the story I had told and the story created by the class with his own world, in which video games most likely play a big part. The story that this student made up was not only quite eloquent but also was better and more powerful than the story created collectively by the class; in the class-created story, there was no direct confrontation between the hero and the witch.

The reaction of this student turned out not to be an isolated incident. In subsequent sessions at different schools, other students with autism responded to the approach I used in the class story-creation session and actively participated. In one instance, a boy with autism showed a lot of interest and enthusiasm during the session and kept offering his ideas for the story being created. At one point, I decided to limit his input and call on other students in the class. The teacher later told me that, after I had switched to the other students, he seemed to withdraw again into his own world.

In both situations described above, the teachers were astounded by the reactions of these children, saying it was the first time they had seen them showing real interest and involvement. However, their response appears to support Bettelheim's claim that children with autism can be reached through fairy tales. Certainly, I have seen that working with fairy tales in conjunction with an interactive approach touches the autistic child—who is drawn in by participating in the class-creation of a similar story.

Although a video game also offers interaction (in that the players move through the spaces at their own speed and by their own actions), they are playing in someone else's landscape, that of the game designer. That world can be so captivating that it is difficult to escape

"I have seen that working with fairy tales in conjunction with an interactive approach touches the autistic child— who is drawn in by participating in the class-creation of a similar story"

from it.[33] Use caution when the children offer up characters from video games when the class is creating their fairy tale. It may not be easy for them to freely invent their own story when they pluck the characters from a game. The game's universe may be so concrete and confining that it prevents the children from accessing their own imaginations.

The session that worked differently

During the process of the story's creation, one idea gives rise to the next one. That cannot happen when the ideas are predetermined at the beginning of the story's creation, as occurred in one class session. At one school, the librarian who had observed the first class session asked to participate in the next class session to try a different strategy. I welcomed her input, so the next session was a joint one. I told the sample fairy tale and demonstrated it on the action-map with the magnetic button-characters. Then I turned the class over to the librarian and I became the observer.

The librarian used an easel with chart paper on which she wrote headings: Where? Who? Grown-ups in Charge, Responsibility, Villain, Magical creature, Help, Magical object. Her strategy was to put down words and ideas first, and then to brainstorm with the children, writing their suggestions underneath the headings, for example:

Where?	Who?	Grown-ups in Charge
hotel	ourselves	teacher
haunted house	girl & boy	aunt/uncle
Edmonton	dog	sister/brother
motel	newspaperman[34]	actor
bad place	crow	grandpa/grandma
graveyard		sick person

Under different circumstances, charting the ideas first in brainstorming fashion is a very effective method. However, listing all ideas before the story's creation takes away the opportunity to reach into a personal experience within the flow of the story. This procedure leaves nothing that can spark a child's imagination, and nothing to which the children can relate their ideas. It also inhibits them from making logical links or unconscious connections with the events in the story, the kind of connections that occur when one word gives rise to the next during the process of creating a new story. Rodari described his personal experience of how a single word took the story in a new direction in the chapter about "recasting" in his book *The Grammar of Fantasy*:

> If I ask myself at which point a spark was ignited and my energy was set into motion to conceive the new story, I can easily respond that it was with the word *oven*. I have already said that I am the son of a baker ... To me, the word *oven* means a large room filled with sacks of flour ...[35]

Rodari could see that the contemporary world, the present reality, will likely make its way into the newly created tale, and new messages will emerge involuntarily and inevitably. It follows, then, that when all the story's ideas are put down *before* rather than during the story's creation, nothing new can emerge.

After listing the words and ideas on the charts, the class voted on them, and the deciding factor was how interesting the idea was on its own without any reference point. The voting process took a long time, during which the spell of the sample story I had told was slowly beginning to dissipate.

After the ideas were chosen, the librarian passed the class back to me to guide the new story creation. The random ideas, now marked with asterisks on the easel, presented a challenge to work with because they resembled a shopping list. The subsequent story creation was a disjointed, bumpy ride and ended as a less satisfying story than those we created in other class sessions. Making the idea charts first was different from plotting a new story together, using the plot that already existed in the action-map and pictographic symbols for the sample tale I had told the class.

The class preparation for the creation of a new story should consist solely of listening to the sample tale. It establishes the mood and casts its spell over the audience. It activates the right side of the brain, which deals with feelings and instincts. Perhaps listening to a story first is what opens the psyche of the audience, who become more attuned to the next step, the creation of a new story. In other words, listening acts as a limbering-up exercise before the dance. When the children are then asked for their ideas during the creation of a new story, that is, while they are immersed in the moment, they respond to what has gone on before instinctively because the story itself leads them on.

Tale Type:
The Animal Bride

This is a tale type with a long tradition, told from at least the Middle Ages. Many of the tales come from Europe, but others I found come from Chile, the Philippines, and Armenia. The main character in these stories is a simpleton, the common and popular hero of folklore, who is usually the third and youngest in the family. Bruno Bettelheim says that a child can easily identify with a third youngest in a fairy tale because, in the most basic family configuration, the child is the third down, regardless of whether he is the oldest, the middle, or the youngest among the siblings or the family members. In the child's mind, the first two are the parents and the third is the child in relation to the parents.[36]

The simpleton character is the one who, at the beginning of the tale, is the least likely to succeed but who, by the tale's end, proves to be the chosen one. This character reminds us of Cinderella, who is overlooked, mocked, and bullied by siblings. Such issues have been central to my choice of this tale type, because it addresses children's similar concerns—feeling neglected, being held in low esteem, having low self-esteem, and being bullied.

For classroom use, I chose a little-known tale from the Brothers Grimm, called "The Poor Miller's Boy and the Little Cat" because it was simple. In many stories of this type, the aging father decides it is time to let one of his sons take over. But first, he wants one of them to prove himself capable and worthy of being his successor, so he sets his sons a difficult task.

In this Grimms' tale, the sons face only one trial, unlike other tales whose protagonists face three trials that are mere repetitions of the first one. The element of time was of some importance to me because I wanted to devote most of my research session with the children to the creation of a new tale. Also, the modern feminist ending of the story appealed to me as a storyteller, and I felt it might have similar appeal to an audience of contemporary children. I describe the ending as "feminist" because the transformed animal/future bride of the simpleton arrives by herself to get her man, then turns down her prospective groom's inheritance, relying instead on her own material means. The changes I made to "The Poor Miller's Boy and the Little Cat" follow:

① In the initial set-up of the story, I substituted a father and his three sons for the miller and his three apprentices because most stories of this tale type have this family relationship.

② Changing the father's profession from miller to farmer saved the time of explaining what a miller is.

③ I shortened the middle part of the story.

④ I injected into my new story three elements from "The Three Feathers," another Grimms' tale belonging to this tale type: i) the name Dummling for the simpleton; ii) the father's ritual of dispatching his sons was a nice element for the children to play with; iii) the hero going underground on his quest because it provided a richer image than remaining aboveground.

The story: "The Farmer's Boy and the Orange Cat"

Once there was a farmer who had three sons. The two older ones were strong and clever, but the youngest one was small and did not talk much. So everyone just called him Dummling. The father was getting old and began to think of his end. One day, he called his sons and said, "Go out into the world and bring me back a horse. Whoever brings the finest of horses will get the farm."

Then he took three feathers, blew them into the air, and said to his sons, "Follow the flight of the feathers." One feather flew to the east, the second flew to the west, and the third one flew straight ahead, but not very far. So, one son went to the left and another went to the right, but before they left, they said to Dummling, "You might as well stay home because you'll never get a horse as long as you live." So Dummling went straight ahead, but after a while he sat down on the ground and was sad.

As he sat there, he noticed the third feather, right next to a trapdoor in the ground. He lifted the trapdoor and saw stairs going deep into the ground. He climbed down the stairs and found another door. When he walked through it, he saw a landscape just like the one above ground. Dummling walked and walked until he was tired. Then he lay down to rest and fell asleep. When he awoke, he saw a little orange cat staring at him.

"I know what you want," said the cat. "You're looking for a horse. If you come and work for me for one year, I will get you that horse." So Dummling followed the cat to her house. There, she gave him a silver axe and asked him to chop some wood. Then, she gave him a silver hammer and nails and asked him to build her a little cottage. And so it went. When the year was over, Dummling asked the cat, "Can I have the horse now?"

The cat told him, "You can see him, but you can't have him yet." She led him to the stable, and there it was—the most beautiful horse Dummling had ever seen. The cat said, "Go home now and in three days, I will bring the horse to you." Then the cat showed him the way back up to the farm.

When Dummling got home, his brothers were already there. Each of them had brought back a horse. "So, where is your horse?" they asked Dummling.

"It's going to be delivered," Dummling answered.

His brothers laughed and said, "Yeah, sure. Where would *you* find a horse? *Of course*, you wouldn't get one." And they did not even let him eat with them or sleep in the house. So Dummling had to stay in the barn.

After three days had passed, a carriage arrived at the farm. A girl with orange hair just like the cat's stepped out of the carriage. She asked to see Dummling. The brothers answered, "You don't want to talk to him." But the girl insisted, so they brought Dummling to her.

Then she asked to see the horses that the brothers had brought. One horse was blind and the other was lame. The girl led forward the horse that she had brought for Dummling. Everyone could see that this horse was the most magnificent horse ever.

The farmer said, "Dummling, the farm is now yours."

But the girl said, "You can keep the horse and the farm because I have a house and I also have a cottage that your son built for me. And that's where we are going." Then she and Dummling climbed into the carriage and drove off.

For the children's subsequent creation of the class story, I retained the masculine gender of the hero and his siblings in order to be consistent with all other stories of this tale type. Also, it was a necessary choice, leading to the modern story-ending where the enchanted animal is transformed into a young woman and comes to get her future groom—the hero. In the classroom session, the children's input begins when they suggest the name for the hero-simpleton and decide upon the father's business.

The actions in the story

"The Farmer's Boy and the Orange Cat"

Here is the sequence of Propp's actions as they appear in this story, with my symbols that represent them.

 I.   Home (additional symbol for beginning or ending of story)

 8a.   Parent needs or desires to have something

 x.   Dispatching ritual (an additional symbol)

9./10. Hero/ine goes or is sent on journey to search for it and bring it back

 11. Hero/ine meets a magical animal or person

TEST 12./13 Hero/ine is tested for kindness and help, and reacts

 20a. Hero/ine returns

 1a. Home (additional symbol for beginning or ending of story)

 23. Hero/ine arrives home unrecognized, unappreciated

**TASK
or
TEST** 25./26. Hero/ine undertakes test or task

        i)   ordeal

        ii) riddle guessing

        iii) choosing

        iv) some other test

 19. The object of the search is obtained, and the spell is broken

27.   Hero/ine is recognized

29.   Hero/ine is given a new
        i)   rank
        ii) appearance
        iii) clothes

31.   Hero/ine is rewarded and/or is married

Action-symbol map of "The Farmer's Boy and the Orange Cat"

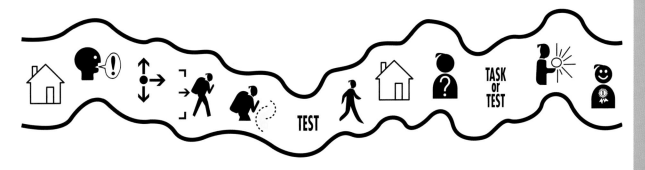

Creating a new story

My research session with this story took place in a public school in Toronto located close to a large park.

My question: What will be the name of the youngest son?

Students' answer: Mark!

(Q) What is the father's job?

(A) *Banker*

(Q) What does the father ask his sons to bring him?

(A) *The biggest money bag*

(Q) How does the father send his sons on the journey? What is the ritual?

(A) *He tossed three coins in the air.*

(Q) Where does it lead Mark? Describe the setting and what happens.

(A) *Mark walks through a park and comes to a tree with a door. He goes inside and falls asleep.*

(Q) Who does Mark meet there? How? (The best is a magical animal.)

(A) *Golden raccoon*

(Q) What kind of work does Mark have to do for the golden raccoon? Describe it.

(A) *Collect garbage*

(Q) How long does Mark work for the raccoon?

(A) *For two years*

(Q) What happens after the work is done?

(A) *The raccoon says to Mark, "I will give you money, but you can't spend it."*

(Q) When does Mark get his reward? Does he get to see it? Where? Describe what happens.

(A) *Mark goes up in the tree, waits for one day, then the golden raccoon brings him a big bag of money.*

Ⓠ What happens when the hero returns home?

Ⓐ *He meets his brothers at the door.*

Ⓠ What did the brothers bring from their journeys? Describe.

Ⓐ *One brother brought fake money and the other one brought chocolate money.*

Ⓠ What is the father's reaction? What does he say? Describe.

Ⓐ *Mark is the winner and he inherits the bank.*

Ⓠ What happens to the magic animal?

Ⓐ *The raccoon goes back to the raccoon world.*

At this point, I started to summarize the story created by the class and asked to be corrected in case I made any mistakes. At the same time as I recounted their story, I moved the magnetic-buttons across the action-symbol map to show the students how their characters progressed through the story. Here is a summary of the story invented by these grade 3 students.

Samples of Children's Stories

Raccoon

There was a father who was a banker, and he had three sons. He wanted to retire. He said to his sons, "Whoever will bring me the biggest money bag will inherit the bank." Then he tossed three coins in the air. Where they fell to the ground indicated which direction the sons had to go.

The youngest of the sons, whose name was Mark, kept walking, and he came to a tree that had a door. He went inside of the tree and fell asleep. When he woke up, he saw a golden raccoon. It was a magical raccoon with golden eyes. The raccoon said to Mark, "Work for me for two years, and you will get a lot of money." Mark had to collect garbage for the raccoon.

When two years were over, the raccoon said to Mark, "I will give you the money, but you can't spend it." Mark goes up in the tree, waits for one day, then the raccoon brings a big bag of money and Mark goes home.

All three brothers meet at the door of their house. Mark has the most money. One brother has fake money, and the other one has chocolate money. Mark is the winner and he inherits the bank. What happened to the raccoon? The raccoon goes back to the raccoon world.

The following are examples of children's stories based on the action-symbol map of "The Farmer's Boy and the Orange Cat."

The Fish

There is a plumber who has three sons and who owns a plumbing shop. He wants one of his three sons to inherit his shop. Because he doesn't know which son should get it, he asks them to bring him a treasure chest with diamonds, gold, and a flower that looks like a poppy, never dies, and you can wish upon it. Then he rolls three pebbles to determine the direction his sons should go.

Joe, his youngest son, follows his pebble, which rolls into a river. Joe sits on a big rock beside the river and sees a fish. The fish offers to help Joe but tells him that he must work for her first. He has to build a bridge over the river, feed her, and clean her teeth.

Joe works for three months and then he wants to see the treasure that he is to get. The treasure is underneath the river, so he has to climb down. He sees the poppy in the middle of the crystals and gold. The fish says, "Go home; the treasure will be delivered to you."

When Joe returns home, his brothers are already there. One brought false treasure, the other one brought a rusty pipe. A few days later, a rainbow-coloured limousine pulls up to the plumbing shop. Out steps a girl. She has a beautiful bag. Inside is the treasure with the never-wilting flower. The father says, "So, Joe, you can now have the shop." And Joe answered, "Okay."

The Candy Shop

A father has three sons and the youngest one is named Jordan. The father owns a candy shop. He is getting old and wants to pass his business to one of his sons. He asks them to bring him a parrot to keep him company in his old age. Then he rolls three balls to show them which way to go.

Jordan's ball rolls into a tunnel. He goes inside and hears something flapping around his head. It is a bat. The bat says, "I know what you want and I can help you if you work for me for one year." He asks Jordan to build him a haunted house.

When the year is over, Jordan wants to get the parrot, but the bat says, "Not yet. It will be a surprise." So Jordan goes back through the tunnel and returns home.

One of his brothers brought a parrot that cannot

speak. The other one brought back a parrot that was muddy and had a broken wing. After a few days, a parrot flies into the candy shop. He is very colourful and has strong wings. He has shiny feathers with sparkles and constantly talks.

The parrot flies into the candy shop saying, "Candy! Candy!" Everyone can see that this is the best parrot. So Jordan inherits the candy shop and his brothers have to work for him as employees from then on.

Discussion of results

Identification with the hero/ine

The choice of the father's profession in the individual story reflects the children's personal lives. For instance, in one of the stories, the father is a tax collector. When I questioned the girl who made that suggestion, she said that her uncle was a tax collector.

Figure 21

Fairy Tales in the Classroom

Some female students identify with the story's male protagonist. In Figure 21, the female student-artist portrays the hero of the story, a boy called Ben; but Ben looks like a girl, judging from the long eyelashes, red lips, and pink shirt with a heart on the front.

Linking the ideas in narrative logic

The spontaneous process of relating one thing to another (cause and effect) gave the narrative a life of its own. The students took the opportunity independently to make a prediction on their own about what could happen next. Because the story was theirs, they were vested in the process and, therefore, they wanted to move the narrative forward. For the adult guiding it, the process involves listening, connecting, and relating, which can induce fears similar to the feeling of walking into a dark tunnel. But that's when the action-symbol map comes into play. It serves as a support one can hold onto so as not to get lost.

I found during the class's story-creating session that I often glanced at the action-symbol map for my own reassurance, to confirm for myself where we were in the story and what action should follow next. The action-symbol map kept me on track, but at the same time allowed me to concentrate fully on what the children were saying. It freed me enough to be one step ahead of the children, to predict in my mind where each suggestion or idea could lead in our story.

In "The Farmer's Boy and the Orange Cat" that I told to the children, the father is a farmer, and he asks his sons to get him a horse—the one who brings the best horse will inherit the farm. On his travels, the hero meets a cat that promises to get him the horse if he serves her for a period of time. The following are samples and a discussion of the logic links in the narratives that developed during the classroom sessions.

Example 1

In one of the class-created stories, the father is a plumber who asks for the biggest pipe, or a toolbox, or a treasure. As you can see, the first two ideas were directly connected to the plumbing profession. However, because I did not accept these for the story right away and allowed the students to vote for their choice, they chose the treasure because it seemed the most magical. The students made the treasure magical indeed, because among the diamonds and gold was a flower that never dies. This suggestion was made by a student about whom later on the librarian said, "Oh, that one ... her parents tell her a lot of stories and she reads a lot." The fact that the flower turned out to look like a poppy did not come as a surprise; it was Remembrance Day, and many of the adults in the school were wearing red poppies in their lapels.

Then, in the class story, the hero finds himself beside a river. He encounters a fish. She asks him to build her a bridge over the river. This request makes quite a bit of sense because, unknown to the hero, the fish is the keeper of the treasure under the river. She would like to have a bridge in order to keep people away from the treasure. The children had no time to think it through, but in retrospect it all fits and makes sense because the children unconsciously linked the ideas in a logical way.

Figure 22

In Figure 22, the student portrays one scene from the story in a collage featuring the story's characters, but adding new elements. We see the two older brothers standing on the left side of the plumber's shop while their father stands on the right, throwing pebbles. The youngest son, Joe, is portrayed as small and insignificant, and he sits on a large rock by the river near the half-constructed bridge he has made. In the river is the talking fish and on the bottom right hand side is the treasure chest with the flower that never dies. Behind the story's characters, the student added a sign with "Fun World," something he invented on his own that was not in the class-created story. It has a park with a playground, a train ride, a jungle, a circus (spelled as "cricus"), and a roller coaster.

When the logic did not quite work

One story in which the internal logic did not quite work was created during my visit to the private school. There, the students in the class were exceptionally mature and competitive with each other and were eager to show off the complexity of their ideas. For the animal that the hero meets, the students suggested a flamingo or an iguana. To a child living in Toronto, both the flamingo and the iguana are overtly exotic animals. By the majority of votes, the iguana made it into the class-created story. When the iguana asked the hero to do a job for her, everybody in the class wanted to be the one in control of the story. The students had the hero travel through volcanoes and lava, swim among crocodiles, and run through laser beams. They also decided that the iguana had to ask the hero to bring a hamburger from the King of Harvey's.

Sending the hero on another journey as a task is an added element to the story's structure that neither the map of symbols nor the sample tale called for. The element of an added journey as a task also came up during my first session with the French Immersion class, but there it was turned down. Because such additions to the story's structural elements happened only in the two most advanced and mature classes,[37] we could say perhaps that enlarging the story's structure can be interpreted as a sign of sophistication and of linguistic maturity.

The students had the story's hero crawl like Spiderman on the wall of the King of Harvey's castle, which they described as taller than the CN Tower. The king himself looked like a giant burger, and so their story continued. In the end, that story turned out to be the least satisfying of all in the second sessions. Why? Because the students' suggestions were too complicated, had too many details, and used images that were mostly man-made. Also, because every student wanted to be a leader, they did not listen very well to the story itself or to one another's suggestions. In the fairy tale, simplicity works better. In other words, less is more. It is the simple, nature-oriented imagery that cuts straight down to the core of the archetype, that resonates with listeners or readers and produces meaning. The students' stories that contain plain and nature-based imagery feel richer, in both scope and scale; thus, they evoke a stronger response. In the story from the students in a private school, the bones of the plot were buried under many complex details and man-made imagery. Although the students exercised their imagination and had opportunities to express themselves throughout their story's creation, their story itself was lost and became meaningless.

"It is the simple, nature-oriented imagery that cuts straight down to the core of the archetype, that resonates with listeners or readers and produces meaning."

Story endings

At the end of the sample story, the hero goes home and awaits the arrival of the horse that the cat had promised. The horse is indeed delivered, but the cat has been transformed into a young woman. The horse she brought for the simpleton hero is clearly the best, so the father decides to pass the farm on to the simpleton. But there is a catch: The cat/woman says to the father, "You can keep the farm, as I have a house of my own, and that's where we are going."

As noted earlier, one of the reasons I selected the tale was for its modern, feminist ending, but there came a surprise! This was not the construct that the children followed in their stories. In fact, the children bypassed the boy-girl union altogether. Instead, in their tales, the hero accepted the father's inheritance, and the brothers were punished, while the magical animal more or less faded into the background or became a friend.

The first time children came up with this type of ending was in a school in Northern Ontario, but I didn't give it any further thought then. In the class-created story, the magic zebra just walked away instead of transforming into a girl, as in the sample story, as if her function had been fulfilled by leading the hero to the treasure.

The second time I used this tale was at a public school in Toronto, and I emphasized in my storytelling the part where the animal returned as a human, a future bride, so the children would not miss it. Again, in the ending of the class-created story, they bypassed the transformation and the upcoming marriage, and they wanted to keep the magical animal out of the story. The children were clearly not interested in turning the animal into a human of the opposite sex, in the "boy meets girl" part of the plot. Even when I specifically asked the children whether they would like to change the animal into something else, their answer was resolutely NO!

When, in my session with the children in the public school, I tried to insist on the transformation, they changed the animal, although the boys protested against turning it into a girl. In the end, however, they made no further change, such as a relationship or a marriage. I realized then that, in a mixed classroom setting where everyone can speak up, I could not negotiate a boy-girl union because it does not interest children of this age.

In research studies by Carolyn Bearse and Elizabeth Yeoman, similar phenomena could be observed in the fairy tales that the students created. In Bearse's study, a student ended his fairy tale with the hero living a happy life with his pet wolf.[38] Similarly, a story created during my research study ended with the hero living with a pet and not, as expected, with a bride. In Yeoman's study, one student ended her story with "Caroline became Henry's tutor, and they lived happily ever after." There was no marriage to follow.[39] Yeoman saw such an ending as the result of the student's exposure to the feminist stories provided by the teacher of the class. However, I suggest that such an ending simply reflects that student's contemporary world, and the student wrote it instinctively to create meaning for herself.

What emerges is that children make sense of stories on their own terms. When creating their own stories, what matters to them most is that justice is done, without concern for boy-girl union or marriage. My observation in this area supports Bettelheim's claim that children relate only to what addresses their inner conflicts and they disregard what they are not ready for.[40] My finding also puts in a new light the feminist worries about the effect that fairy tales with their happily-ever-after endings has on children as being their own concerns, unfounded in the reality of children's worlds. As for the concept of justice, often the punishments that children meted out to the villains in their stories were certainly "cruel and unusual," which confirms the sense of retributive justice that children of this age desire at this stage of their psychological development.

Tale Type: Magic Objects

Many stories from around the world belong to this tale type. Some are quite long and complex, but the general pattern remains the same: A magical object is acquired in some extraordinary manner; the hero or heroine uses the object and, through it, he or she gains wealth and status; then someone who is envious steals the magical object and the hero has to get it back.

I chose this tale type for my research because it touches upon the issues of envy and honesty, issues that directly concern children. In some stories, the magical object produces a quantity of food. Because food holds a major appeal for children, I focused on stories of this type when I selected the sample tale for the classroom. Also, excitement is generated by a disaster such as when the food uncontrollably multiplies.

Out of the three tale types I selected for the classroom, this type had the most complex plot structure. It had two parts that could exist independently as separate stories. In the first part, as in the story "The Magic Porridge Pot" by the Brothers Grimm, the heroine under mysterious circumstances acquires the magical object that solves her problem. There is no jealous villain and the food disaster is created by a mother's ignorance. In the second part, the jealous villain makes his entry after the protagonist acquires the magical object.

Initially, the story "The Magic Porridge Pot" alone seemed most appropriate for the classroom, but other stories contained several elements that I wanted to include in my version, so I wove a hybrid of them all for storytelling in the classroom. At first, I wanted to honour the most popular story of this tale type, "The Magic Porridge Pot," by keeping "porridge" in the sample story, but I soon discovered that few children today have any idea what porridge is.[41] So I resolved the problem by having the pot produce soup instead and, accordingly, the story has been called "The Magic Soup Pot."

The story: "The Magic Soup Pot"

In a village there lived a poor man whose only possessions were a house with a leaky roof and a goat. When he had nothing left to eat at home, he decided to go to the town nearby and sell his goat in the market.

As he walked through the woods, he felt hot and tired so he sat down in the shade to rest. It was exactly noon. Suddenly an old woman appeared, dressed in rags like a beggar.

"Good day!" she said. "Where are you going?" The man told her he was off to sell his goat as he had nothing left to eat at home.

"I can help you," the woman said. She pulled out a rusty pot from her bag. "I can trade you this pot for your goat. You will not regret it. All you have to do is say to it, 'Cook, pot! Cook!' and it will cook a delicious soup for you. When you have enough, just say to it, 'Stop, pot! Stop!' and it will stop cooking. But don't tell anyone about it!"

So the man traded his goat for the pot, and the woman vanished as suddenly as she had appeared.

When the man returned home, he put the pot on the table and said to it, "Cook, pot! Cook." And before you could count to ten, the pot was full of soup. "Stop, pot! Stop!" the man commanded, and it stopped filling. Then he ate his soup and was happy, because he would never be hungry again.

A few days later a neighbour was passing by his house. Through the window, she smelled the delicious soup. "How come," she wondered, "this poor man can afford such a delicious meal?" She knocked on the door and invited herself in. The man shared his soup with her as she pried and asked him questions. Finally, the man told her about the magic pot.

"And all you have to do is to say, 'Cook, pot! Cook!' Right?" she said, just to make sure. She couldn't get the pot out of her mind.

Next time the man went out for a walk, the neighbour sneaked in with her own rusty pot and exchanged it for the magic one. She took it home and said to it, "Cook, pot! Cook." And sure enough, soup began bubbling in the pot. It rose so quickly that the pot was nearly full. "I must get a plate and spoon," she said. When she returned, the soup was already pouring out of the pot, over the table, and onto the floor. She didn't know how to stop it, so she put the plate on top of the pot. But it fell off, and the soup just kept flowing. Soon her whole house was full of soup.

To save herself from drowning, the neighbour climbed up on the roof. "Help!" she called as the soup was pouring out of the door and onto the road like a river.

Just then, the poor man was coming back to his house. He realized what had happened. "Please, make the pot stop!" the neighbour begged the man. So he called out, "Stop, pot! Stop." And the river of soup stopped rising.

It took the neighbour weeks of hard work to clean up her house, all slimy from the soup. As for the man, he got his pot back and was never hungry again.

The actions in the story

Here is the sequence of Propp's actions as they appear in this story, with my symbols that represent them.

 1.   Home (additional symbol for beginning or ending of story)

 8a.   Someone in the family desires to have something

 9./10.   Hero/ine goes or is sent on a journey to search for it and bring it back

 11.   Hero/ine meets a magical animal or person

TEST   12./13. Hero/ine is tested for kindness and help and reacts

 14.   Hero/ine is rewarded by magical thing/s

20a. Hero/ine returns

31. Hero/ine is rewarded and/or is married

 4. Villain asks question about the object, person he wants to get

 5. Villain gets the information

INFORMATION

EMERGENCY 8. Villain steals the object or abducts a person

TASK
or
TEST
25./26. Hero/ine undertakes test or task

 30. Villain or impostor is punished

Action-symbol map of "The Magic Soup Pot"

Creating a new story

This classroom session took place in a public school in mid-town Toronto. All children were grade 3 students.

My question: Who will be the main character? A boy, a girl, a man, or a woman?

Students' answer: *A boy!*

Ⓠ What will be his name?

Ⓐ *Andrew*

Ⓠ Who does Andrew live with?

Ⓐ *His father*

Ⓠ What do Andrew and his father need?

Ⓐ *Pizza*

Ⓠ Which of his possessions is Andrew going to sell so he can buy the pizza?

Ⓐ *His martial arts/karate medal*

Ⓠ Where is Andrew going to sell it?

Ⓐ *He goes into town.*

Ⓠ Whom does Andrew meet along the way?

Ⓐ *He meets an old man.*

Ⓠ What's unusual about this man? What does he look like? Describe him.

Ⓐ *He looks like a pizza.*

Ⓠ What does the man offer to Andrew for the martial arts medal?

Ⓐ *A seed of a magic pizza tree.*

Ⓠ What is Andrew to do with the seed? Are there any special instructions?

Ⓐ *Put the seed in the ground and water it with only one cup of water.*

Ⓠ What happens after that?

Ⓐ *Andrew trades in his medal, puts the seed carefully in his pocket, and goes back home. He plants it in the garden and waters it the way the*

old man told him. Soon the tree grows, looking like a Christmas tree
but full of pizzas.

ⓠ Who gets jealous and wants a pizza tree like that, too?
Ⓐ *A neighbour who lives on a farm.*

ⓠ What does the neighbour do?
Ⓐ *He steals the seeds.*

ⓠ Where are the seeds?
Ⓐ *A special pizza on top of the tree has the seeds.*

ⓠ How does the neighbour get them?
Ⓐ *He sends his special flying chicken at night to steal the seed-pizza.*

ⓠ What happens after the neighbour gets the seed-pizza?
Ⓐ *He plants the seed-pizza in the ground and waters it a lot with a hose*
and a sprinkler.

ⓠ What sort of emergency does that create?
Ⓐ *Too much water, too many pizza trees! The neighbour's farm overflows*
with pizzas and the neighbour cannot stop it.

ⓠ Is Andrew able to stop the pizzas from coming?
Ⓐ *Andrew calls, "Magical tree, stop making pizzas!"*

ⓠ How do the neighbour farmer and his chicken get punished?
Ⓐ *They have to eat all the pizzas and they get a stomach-ache. They*
have to clean up the farm.

At this point, I re-tell their story for the class, and ask them to correct me
if I make any mistakes. At the same time, I move the magnetic button-
characters along the path on the symbol map to show the class how
the characters progress throughout their invented story. Here is the
summary of their story:

The class-created story: "Pizza Tree"

Once there was a father with a son whose name was Andrew. One day they really wanted to have a pizza, but there was no money in the house to buy it. So Andrew took his martial arts medal and went to town to sell it. As he walked, he met an old man who kind of looked like a pizza. The old man offered to buy Andrew's medal and gave him, in return, the seed of a pizza tree.

He told him, "Put the seed in the ground and water it with only one cup of water." Andrew put the seed carefully in his pocket and went back home. He planted the seed in the garden and watered it the way the old man told him. Soon the tree grew out of the ground, looking like a Christmas tree but hung with pizzas. On the top of the pizza tree was a special pizza, which contained the seeds.

Andrew's neighbour wanted a tree like that, too. So he sent his special flying chicken at night to steal the pizza with the seeds at the top of the tree. He planted that pizza in his own garden and he watered it for a long time with a hose and a sprinkler. Too much water, too many pizzas. The neighbour's farm began to over-flow with pizzas and no one could stop it. The grease of the cheese made the road and the ground slippery.

Andrew saw what was happening and commanded, "Magical tree, stop making pizzas!" The farmer and his chicken got punished by having to eat all of the pizzas. They both got a stomach-ache. They also had to clean up their farm.

Other samples of children's stories

The following two class-created stories are also based on the action-symbol map of "The Magic Soup Pot."

The Magic Sewing Machine

Benny lives in a cottage in the mountains. Winter is coming and he needs warm clothes, as his old ones are falling into shreds. Benny takes his book and walks for a long time down the mountain. Then he meets an old woman. She trades her sewing machine for his book and she tells him, "All you have to do is say to it, 'Sew, machine. Sew.' To stop it, you must tell it, 'Stop, sewing machine.'" She tells Benny to keep it a secret.

One day, Benny's sister comes to visit Benny in the mountains. She cannot believe her eyes, seeing all of the beautiful clothes Benny has there. She is into fashion, so she inquires where Benny got all of those clothes. Finally, Benny tells her about the sewing machine and how it works.

The next time Benny's sister comes to visit, she brings her own sewing machine and switches it for Benny's. When she returns home, she tries it and pricks her finger on the sewing machine's needle and bleeds to death.

Magic Glasses

Jack needs new eyeglasses. He goes to town to buy them. In the park by a tree, he meets a glowing old lady. He buys glasses from her. The glasses are not ordinary but are magical and allow him to see the future. The glasses let him see the numbers of the lottery. He buys the ticket with the numbers, wins the lottery, and becomes rich.

His best friend finds out and becomes jealous. When he comes to see Jack, he exchanges the glasses. Then he puts them on and cannot take them off. The glasses only fit the person to whom they were given. He calls for help. The police come and try to take the glasses off but nothing works. Only Jack can take the glasses off. His friend cannot see well anymore and he goes blind.

Discussion of results

Although the children personalized their stories and imbued them with meaning, the stories themselves, in comparison to the ones from the other two tale types, were more mundane. The reasons for this seem to be that

- the plot structure of the story is more complex because it consists of two parts.
- the story does not take place in a magic realm as the stories of the other two tale types do. There is no talking animal and the only interesting thing here is that the desired object itself can magically multiply.

This, however, is not very interesting for children to draw. Drawing the same object over and over again to show how the thing multiplies seems more like a form of punishment than a fun activity. The villain, by being an ordinary human (a relative or a neighbour), did not engage the children's imagination as much as the fantasy villain in our first session's story.

After a couple of sessions, when I realized that the ordinary characters were not very interesting for the children to draw, I presented the story in such a way that the protagonist would have to meet an unusual character. In one instance, this gave rise to a light-emitting, glowing old woman, an appropriate image for a story in which the hero needed glasses and she could provide them (see Figure 23).

Figure 23

The student drew the glowing woman with a witch's hat to inform us that the woman possessed magical powers. Perhaps in the student's mind, that explained how she came to have the "future-seeing" glasses in her possession.

Children making meaning

In the sample story, the hero needs food. He decides to sell his goat so that he can buy some food. In one class-created story, the hero needs pizza, a TV ("Everybody needs a TV," as students put it), and glasses. The pizza, TV, and glasses are modern things, reflecting contemporary life. In two inner-city schools, the hero needs new clothes, instead. Their re-creation of the story provided the children with the opportunity to express their ideas about what is desirable and important to them, and their choices were influenced by their demographics.

The magic's logic

In the sample story, the hero traded his goat for a magic pot to which he could say, "Cook, pot, cook," and it made as much soup as he desired. The pot made soup, but the "magic" gave the pot the ability to do it at any time and without any ingredients. The magical objects that the children chose and the way the objects were used in the class-created stories manifest the internal logic in the same way as in the traditional folktales. In the children's story, the fantastic properties of such objects are mere exaggerations, magnifications of the properties the real objects have.

For instance, when the hero trades his martial arts medal for a seed, the seed grows into a pizza tree, hung with pizzas. In another class story, the hero buys magical glasses from a glowing old lady and the glasses allow him to see into the future. He can see what the winning numbers in the lottery will be, wins the jackpot, and acquires sudden wealth.

In two of the public schools where the children came up with the same idea—that the hero needs new clothes—the children also made the same logical link: In one story, the hero receives a magical sewing machine that can produce clothing continuously; in another, while the hero chants, "Sew, sew, sew me some clothes," old clothes must be fed into the machine—in some fashion, it is the process of recycling.

The story-creating activity allows the children to venture one step further with the knowledge they have about something such as a seed, glasses, or a sewing machine and take it to previously untested grounds.

The villain's punishment

The magic object elevates the hero into an enviable position, but then the magic object is stolen from the hero by a jealous villain or by an ordinary human being such as a neighbour, brother, sister, or friend. Because the villain does not have the complete instructions to use the magic object properly, a disaster occurs and only the hero can stop it. In my sample story, the villain's household belongings became spoiled as a punishment for his stealing the magic pot. In most cases, the children devised punishments in their stories that were far more severe.

Figure 24

In one child's illustration for the class story (see Figure 24), the hero shrinks his brother for stealing the bracelet of stones.

Figure 25

In another story, the best friend who stole the magic glasses goes blind (Figure 25). Although this may seem like a severe punishment, it fits the crime because it reflects the nature of the stolen object.

Figure 26

In a story about new clothes, the sister who stole the hero's magic sewing machine pricks her finger on it and bleeds to death. Again, the internal logic is at play—the sister is being punished by the stolen object itself.

Figure 27

Another student from the same class added a witch's hat on the sister, perhaps to identify her as an evil character.

G.K. Chesterton once remarked that children are innocent, which is why they love justice, while adults are wicked and naturally prefer mercy.[42] Piaget's research showed that children believed "that justice was most just when it was most severe."[43] The 6- to 8-year-olds do not consider motivation or circumstances in meting out justice and imposing punishment. I tried on several occasions to reason with the children to come up with less severe forms of punishment, but my reasoning went right over their heads because, at their particular developmental stage, they do not feel the same way about it. It is the deed that matters to them, and they judge it by its material results, not by the intentions behind it. By imposing a severe punishment, the children feel the pleasure of revenge in a way that does not cause them any anxiety. Their created stories allow them the opportunity to express feelings of catharsis and, as a result, provide relief from inner tension.

Sessions with older students

On some occasions, I was asked to conduct my story sessions with older students or adults. In spite of my initial concerns that my method might not engage them, I found that these students, too, were eager to play along and participated with enthusiasm. Yet, there was a marked difference in the re-created stories that the older students produced. They lacked charm, had too many complicated man-made images, and offered no magical solutions for the problems of the protagonists. The older students' ideas and solutions to their hero's problems were realistic, reflecting the shifting of their interest toward the real world.

For example, in a story created by grade 5 students, the hero's most precious possession is stolen by the villain. The precious object is a wallet with money, an I.D. card, and a driver's licence. In another story, also created by grade 5 students, the protagonist is a middle-aged woman who needs food, money, and a house to live in. The woman meets a magical girl and asks her for help. The magical girl offers the woman a job. Another student's suggestion was that the woman should get a husband. These older children were trying to work out a situation by providing realistic solutions.

In a story-creation session with undergraduate university students, the hero comes to a tree. The tree asks the hero for help because the townspeople want to cut it down. The hero chains himself to the tree in order to save it. Chaining yourself to a tree is not a magical act—it is a realistic solution to the problem, a solution often performed by student activists, and it expresses their ecology-oriented concerns. The older the students get, the harder it is for them to invent magical solutions. In sessions with adults, everything, including the villain, tends to be reality-based. It appears, then, that if the imagination is not exercised, it will waste away.

"The older the students get, the harder it is for them to invent magical solutions. In sessions with adults, everything, including the villain, tends to be reality-based."

Story endings

While the endings grade 3 students provided to their stories were harsh or violent, the older students were capable of making peaceful resolutions without any guidance from adults. For example, the villain in one story is a bald and toothless animal catcher. He steals animals and skins them to make a fur covering for his bald head. In the story, the hero performs a task that gives the villain hair and wooden teeth. Now that the villain likes the way he looks, he stops being evil. He opens an adoption agency for lost animals and arranges for the animals to go to new homes.

In another story, a lonely giant-villain steals the hero's teddy bear. When the hero accomplishes a task that the villain sets for him, the villain gives the teddy bear back to the hero. Instead of being punished for his crime, as would have happened in a story invented by younger children, the villain asks the hero if he can become his friend so he can join him and not be lonely anymore. Interestingly, the magical characters, the bear and the giant, were suggestions that came from younger students in grade 4, while the peaceful ending was provided by older students in grade 6.

Although the story-creating session does not give older students as many benefits as it gives to younger ones who are more attuned to the imaginary, doing the activity with them is still worthwhile. The students are given the opportunity to practice their social awareness, and they are able to express their views within the safety of the story structure. The activity shows them that fixed narrative can be questioned and that, by asking questions, they can find the answers themselves.

Finally, inventing stories offers a natural transition into more formal writing tasks. Gordon M. Pradl, educator and author of many publications on teaching and literacy, notes that the moral, or point, of a story is what gets eventually transformed into the thesis statement in expository and persuasive essays.[44]

Recollections

Three weeks after the session in the classroom, the teachers did recollection tests of the "story told" and the "story made up" with their students. Prior to the recollection test, they gave no clues to the students and did not hold any discussions.

When recollecting their stories, the children made fewer errors and remembered the majority of details because they had participated in the story's creation and contributed their own ideas. They also expressed more interest in writing about their own stories, judging by the length of their written recollections. I concluded that the personal involvement of the students in the story's creation had helped children to retain the details of the story and also made the story more interesting for them to describe.

An additional observation made during verbal recollections was that the students showed an increased level of enthusiasm in their responses. All hands shot up in the air because everyone wanted to speak; the noise level increased, and the atmosphere in the classroom suddenly became charged with excitement. The children were eager to talk about the "story made up" in their classrooms. Their enthusiastic response was most likely a result of their having had an active role in the story's creation; it made them feel empowered and important.

I liked everything in the story

Expressing Response through Drawing

When present in a classroom of 7- to 9-year-olds, one is struck by the spontaneity, enthusiasm, and joy they exhibit when asked to express themselves through drawing. The children draw with ease, translating into pictures how they visualize the story in their imaginations, and adding extra things on their own to scenes from the story. A close study of the children's drawings about the class-created story reveals a lot of meaning and information that the children would not have been able to express in words.

Because I used no illustrations or photographs as visual aids during the storytelling session, the children had to invent from within when they created their drawings. By not using visual references when telling the tales, we provide open and invaluable space for encouraging students to exercise their imagination.

Same story, different interpretations

In a class story modelled on the structure of "The Magic Soup Pot," the hero encounters a woman who trades him a stone bracelet for his book of golden letters. Here, the same scene is portrayed by three different students:

Figure 28

This student visualized the scene taking place in the city and at night. The woman wears a red-hooded robe, perhaps to make her look mysterious.

Figure 29

Another student's interpretation has the scene set outdoors in nature on a sunny day. Both the hero and the woman are wearing glasses and modern clothes. The woman is handing the stone bracelet to the hero, saying, "here you go," just like a salesperson in a store passing over the purchase to the customer.

Figure 30

The third student portrayed the characters as people of colour. The woman dressed in ragged clothes engages in conversation with the hero. Their dialogue is contained in the bubbles and numbered 1, 2, 3, 4, to tell us in which order the characters speak.

Combining images with textual information

Even though I never ask for it, more than half of the children include in their pictures some form of writing, most often in bubbles containing written comments or dialogue, a convention used in comics and cartoons.

Figure 31

The scene above, from the class story modelled on "The Farmer's Boy and the Orange Cat" sample tale, shows the great finale. Jordan, the youngest son and the story's hero, inherits his father's candy store. His two brothers have to work for him and, most importantly, are not allowed to eat candy. The student added what each character, including the parrot, is thinking.

How children portray stories

As a picture-book author/illustrator, I know how difficult it is to condense a story into a limited number of still pictures. One often has to go on instinct about which images are the crucial ones to tell the story and express the story's meaning. So naturally it was interesting to investigate which one scene out of the entire story the children would portray, having been given total freedom of choice. In their drawings, the majority of children chose to portray a scene set in the magic realm because they found it the most interesting.

Figure 33

This picture shows the climactic scene, the villain's demise while the hero and his sister look on. Golem melted into a puddle in the river of lava, and all that is left of him is an arm.

Figure 34

The artist created a very atmospheric picture. The hero is about to free his dog, which the witch had stolen, from the cage while the witch is inside her hut cooking. Underneath the sad, stooped tree are more cages with imprisoned pets and a pile of bones, remnants of dead pets. Even the sky is black and heavy from the sadness that pervades the whole picture.

Figure 35

I could not resist including this picture. In the story, the hero becomes invisible but the hot dog does not. Thus, the evil wizard could catch the invisible hero by following the floating hot dog. This oversight was not a part of our plot, and I had not realized it until I saw the student's picture! The wizard calls out in an added speech balloon from his dwelling that is five stories high and shaped as a hot dog.

Although I instruct the children to draw a scene from our class-created tale, not all the children do. Some children show only characters of the story, while others may draw pictures as a map of the story, or as a sequence of a few of the incidents from the story, as in storyboarding.

Figure 36

I liked everything in the story

The brother

The student drew the main events of the story in a linear form, as a sequence of incidents. Interestingly, the house on the left side and the house on the right side of the picture resemble symbols on the story map, but here the student made the houses inhabited, as seen by the smoke pouring out of the chimneys. Starting on the left, we see the hero leave home. Next comes the scene of the hero trading his book for the stone bracelet. In the centre of the picture, there is a big television set that the hero desired, and behind it is his new house with a swimming pool, all obtained by the hero's use of the magic bracelet. We see the villain/brother stealing the bracelet and the disaster (many houses piled up in a heap) resulting from the bracelet's misuse. Finally, we see the hero with the magic bracelet back in his possession, punishing his brother for the theft by shrinking him in size.

Recollection through visual expression

Interestingly, some students combined words and pictures in their recollections.

Figures 37 and 38

One student created both of the drawings. The drawing on the left (Figure 37) is the scene the student drew in the first class session. The drawing on the right (Figure 38) was done three weeks later as a recollection of the class-created story. The student remembered the story, but because he had difficulty expressing himself in written form, he used a drawing to communicate it.

Perhaps other children who struggle with their nascent literary expression could confidently express themselves through their drawings if they were given the opportunity to do so. Then, their "response to text" could be assessed in this alternative form. When allowed such alternative expression, many children's problems of self-esteem or even some learning disabilities could be better addressed.[45]

Unfortunately, the spontaneity and ease of drawing so characteristic of this particular age does not last. Howard Gardner notes in his book *Artful Scribbles* that as children get older and more mature, their "drawings exhibit less flavour and increasingly taste the same."[46] The sameness or the lack of original drive in visual expression is attributed to children's heightened interest in realism as they mature.

Right-brain and left-brain modes

There are two modes of information processing in the human brain. The left side of the brain makes rational conclusions based on logic. It analyzes, counts, verbalizes, and marks time and sequences in a linear way. The left side of the brain is digital and objective, and it is where arithmetic and mathematical computations are performed.

The right side of the brain is intuitive, subjective, holistic, and time-free. It relates to the now rather than to the future. The right side of the brain makes us dream, understand metaphors, create new combinations of ideas. It is nonverbal and deals with feelings. It can see how things relate to each other and how the parts fit into a whole. The imagination resides in the right side of the brain and is activated from there.

Around age 5, children begin to draw, to tell stories, to portray their feelings, and to work out their problems. They do so by exaggerating basic forms in their drawings, such as making things very small or big, to express their intended meanings. Once the feeling is drawn, translated into a visual form on the paper, the children may be better able to cope with their problem. Their drawing is spontaneous and they do not make judgments about whether the picture looks right or wrong. Pablo Picasso once said, "Every child is an artist. The problem is how to remain an artist once he grows up."

As children mature and their interest shifts toward realism, they begin to look at their drawing also from a realistic point of view. They start to ask themselves if the object in the drawing looks real. Perhaps it is then that self-consciousness begins to develop and fear of failure takes root. Drawing may no longer provide release or be experienced as a joyful activity, but it may become something of a test. For some children, if their artwork is not met with the approval of peers, drawing may become something to be dreaded.

In our culture, "most of our educational system has been designed to cultivate the verbal, rational, on-time left hemisphere, while the right part of the brain of every student is virtually neglected."[47] Gardner states that "once writing mechanics and literary accomplishments have advanced sufficiently … the stage is set for the decline—or demise— of graphic expression."

Even though spontaneity in drawing declines as children mature and their literary abilities get stronger, the skill of expression in drawing can be maintained simply through continuous use. We call ourselves a visual society because we look at print or fleeting photographic images on a television or computer screen. Ironically, if we were required to express ourselves through drawing, a majority of us would be at a loss. If drawing were endorsed as a basic skill like reading, writing, and arithmetic, then graphic artistry and art appreciation in our culture could be improved.

Summary: Where to Go from Here

My approach to writing stories has real possibilities for primary school curricula—many expectations/outcomes for language study (listening, speaking, reading, writing) can be accomplished through my approach in a unit on fairy tales.

Integration into curriculum expectations

Oral communication
- Contributing ideas, making inferences and predictions, and listening to the ideas of others in the course of the interactive class session
- Extending understanding by connecting ideas to a child's own knowledge and personal experiences, or to other media texts and to the world around them
- Using interactive strategies by making connections in the story and linking children's own responses to what other students say during the story-creating activity
- Using and comprehending the action-symbols and the story map
- Retelling the class-created story in sequence

Writing

- Developing ideas
- Creating a story's characters, setting, problem, and resolution
- Organizing ideas in a logical sequence by presenting a story with a beginning, a middle, and an end, which is accomplished through exposure to and absorption of the action-symbol maps of the tales read to them
- Creating an original story, modelled on the tale told to them. This can lead to students writing stories individually, then to revisions, drafts, publishing, and producing finished works in the form of picture books

Media literacy

- Students choose a scene from the class-created story, visualize the details, and express their interpretation through drawing.
- Children can prepare a storyboard of their entire class-created story.
- They can add sound effects to the story to produce a skit or a play.
- They can re-tell the class-created story from different points of view.

In other research studies such as that of Bearse and Yeoman, the children's class-created stories were the result of a concentrated study of the fairy-tale genre that lasted several months. In my approach, the children's stories are created within one hour-long session because my method engages the students more directly.

Sample follow-up initiatives

Several teachers who witnessed the class sessions took their own initiative and created projects in their classrooms using the story-map action-symbols and the strategies I had used in the session. In both follow-up cases described, they kept the three aspects critical to the method's success:

① **Permission** (to play with and alter the story)
② **Opportunity** (provided in the classroom)
③ **Guidance** (the action-symbol map and the guiding questions)

The teachers also presented their initiatives in the form of playful activities or games. For instance, one teacher enlarged and photocopied the symbols and displayed them on the classroom walls in the sequence of the tale told. He then organized the children in groups of five and asked each group to create their own story, using the action-symbol map. Afterwards, they dramatized their group-created stories and performed them as plays for the rest of their class.

The teacher later gave me the stories that the groups had created and written up. In one story, the writer of the group switched from third person narration into first person in the middle of the story, although the story had been created by the group. Here are some snippets from it:

> One day there was two sisters and their mother told them not to go outside because the hooded fangs will get the little sister and take her to his cave After she found her sister in a cage and when I was going to get the sister I saw the hooded fang Then the mother came home with a bag of chips but the little sister got more chips than the big sister so I grabed it from her and I was happy because she dident cry so my mom dident

hear us and I don't like when she hears me because then I would get in truble.

Another teacher at another school created a handout sheet with Guiding Questions (below) to help the students invent their own individual stories, which they then turned into illustrated booklets.

Create your own Magical Story using the same outline as author Veronika Martenova Charles.

Where does your story take place? It must start off and end in a peaceful place.

Who is the main character of your story?

What is the main character's name?

What responsibility does the main character have?

Who is the one to give the main character instructions on his/her responsibility?

Who is the villain?

What is the villain's name?

What problem does the villain create for the main character?

Who does the main character help along the way?

How does the main character help him/her?

What magical gift does he/she give the main character to thank the main character for helping?

How do the main character and the villain meet?

How does the magical gift help the main character?

How does the story end?

After each student made an outline with his/her own ideas, they proceeded to write a rough copy that was then corrected by the teacher. After the experience of the initial class session, the children seemed to create their individual stories effortlessly. Then, in the following weeks, the students developed their stories into fully illustrated and bound booklets that were put on display at the end of the school year.

Sample individual student stories

With the teacher's permission, I have included the following samples of the students' stories. Although these stories are twice removed from the original story told in the first classroom session, the structure of the story told is still clearly visible.

The Cruise

Once there was a girl named Hannah. She was at a hotel with her Mom and Dad and little brother. One day her Mom and Dad were going to the beach together. They put Hannah in charge of her little brother Zack. Hannah did as she was told. After a while she got bored. So she went out and played tennis with her friends.

Her brother didn't like it. He went out the back. Then this little mean boy came up to him and said, "I dare you to sneak aboard the cruise on the beach!" Her brother said "no." Then the mean boy d-double dared him. Her brother said "ok fine!"

After a while Hannah saw some men selling pictures of the cruise so she went and bought one for only 75 cents. When she got to the hotel she looked at the picture and saw (Oh! No!) her brother in it. By then the cruise was gone and out of sight. Luckily it said where the cruise was going in a corner of the picture. So she set off to look for St. Joe's Island. On the way she saw a cat meowing. She went over to him. He said to pull the thorn out of his paw. So she did. The cat said "thank you." "Since you helped me I will help you! Here is a piece of magic fur. Rub it when you are in danger." So she took it and started walking again. Finally she came to St. Joe's Lake. Then she saw a man with an old row boat. She asked "Can I borrow your boat?" The man said "ok." So she set off. Finally she came to the island.

She walked around for a while then finally she found her brother. She started to run. Then the mean boy saw and started running after her. Then she remembered the magic piece of fur. She pulled it out of her pocket and started rubbing it. Then a big huge root popped up in front of the boy. Then he tripped over it. Hannah quickly put her brother in the boat and started rowing. She finally got to land. When she got home her parents were just pulling the car in the driveway. After that her parents gave her a conche shell for taking care of her brother.

The End

The Oranges

A long time ago in 1999 there was a girl and a boy. Their names were Charles and Victorya. They had a very annoying sister. One day their sister told them to get some oranges for supper. So off they went hand in hand to the town square.

On their way they met a three year old. He had lost his way. Victorya and Charles brought him home and he gave them a bunch of scary beasts. "What can we use them for?" asked Charles. But the three year old was already gone. He didn't even tell us his name" said Victorya. "Oh well" said Charles. So on they went.

After a while Victorya and Charles started to study the beasts. They had long skinny noses and they were very slimy. They also hated teenagers. How could a three year old get these?" Charles said. "I don't know" said Victorya. When they got to the store Simone, Simon and Norman ran up to them. Simone was their sister and the rest were her friends. "Oh no!" moaned Victorya. It was too late! The teenagers squirted them with orange juice. But then the beasts came and scared them away.

Charles and Victorya bought the oranges and went home to change their wet clothes. But after the beasts scared the teenagers they disappeared to never come back again.

The End

The Day Bob Saved the Only Smartie Flavoured Donut

Once there was a policeman named Bob. He loved donuts. He was bald and little fat. He had a good life until the Police Chief told him the only smartie flavoured donut was stolen by evil ninja chicken named Porky! So he started tracking the evil ninja chicken.

While he was tracking he found a donut that didn't have any sprinkles! "You poor little thing", said Bob to the donut. So he went to a donut store and bought some sprinkles. Then he put them on the donut. The donut said thanks to Bob and gave him a bag of golden donuts that when you eat them you gain 1,000,000 pounds. Bob kept tracking until he found the chicken's evil lair.

The ninja chicken started chasing Bob. Bob threw the magic donuts and Porky ate them. Because of all the weight he sank into the middle of the earth.

The End

Follow-up ideas

You will come up with your own follow-up activities after your students invent their story, but here are a few of my suggestions:

① **Your class-created story could be viewed as a first draft.**
The students can then individually write it out or storyboard it. At that point, the children will need your help with descriptive writing and dialogue to develop the story further. The students could stretch and enlarge with details the parts of the story that they particularly like.

② **The students could retell/rewrite/redraw the class-created story from the perspective of another character's perspective.**

One might choose the villain's point of view? Or another might see it through the eyes of the magic creature the hero/ine meets along the way?

③ **The class-created story could become the launching pad for knowledge-building.**

If the story's hero/ine crosses into a magical realm, the children could design how that magical realm would look. Are there plants and animals? What kind? This could lead to nature study. Or, maybe the landscape in the magic realm is as barren as Mars appears. What would that be like? The children could do their research in books about planets and astronomy.

When the story's hero has to work for the magic animal to build a bridge, for instance, this situation could lead the students into research about bridges and building materials. The children could work in groups and then present their findings to the rest of the class.

Because the class-created story is the students' very own, they will view the knowledge gained with heightened interest, and that knowledge once acquired will be remembered because it is tied to their story.

Teachers' follow-up initiatives indicate that the approach outlined in my research study would most likely be used as a springboard for writing stories. This approach can provide the answer to students' most often asked question: "What can I write about?" The strategies offered in my approach provide an easier entry into story-creation, and they help students produce concrete results, something they can show their parents.

Ideally, though, this approach should be used for thinking of a story and visualizing it. If the story can be visualized, then it can be described in any form of expression—spoken or written words, pictures, dramatic play, or even song or dance. In later drafts or versions, the craft of writing and revising to improve clarity, grammar, and mechanical aspects can be stressed.

Learning the craft of expression without having anything to say is a hollow activity. Writing is not about how many words you can put down. It is about what you say and how you say it. Students' interest in expressing their ideas and sharing them with others through writing is inevitably followed by an increased desire to learn how to do it well.

Educators are aware of the importance of intuitive and creative thought, but need to nourish much more the right brain, the hemisphere of the dreamer and the artist. We all long to be creative, but imagination feeds on art and on stories. Only after it is fed, can the imagination create its own artwork and narrative.

My recommendation from my research study is that primary students be given more opportunities to engage their imagination, express their creativity, and construct their own meaning through recreating fairy tales and retelling them in their own stories. My hope is that, ultimately, the children will develop and sustain their ability to see themselves as heroes of the exciting stories of their own lives.

TEST
Ratburn River
anne
Magic stick
tree with
big leaves
SHOPPERS
DRUG MART

Putting My Approach into Practice

If you came straight to this section, your enthusiasm for getting started is commendable. To bring you up to speed, here is a brief summary of how to use fairy tales with the approach described in this book. However, if you have read the preceding chapters, you already know it all—but it is always good to review.

General description of my approach

These are key words that will ensure success with this approach:

Permission (to play with story)
Opportunity (provided in the classroom)
Guidance (by an adult and the action-symbol map of the
tale's structure)

This is a story-building activity using maps of fairy tale structures as a guide. The adult and the children work collaboratively to create a new story. The adult initiates the story, poses non-leading questions and then, listening carefully to the children's ideas and suggestions, responds, and guides the children in the direction they wish to go. After each idea or suggestion is chosen, the adult makes the idea concrete by putting it into sentence and tying it into the developing story. Because this is an improvisational activity, there has to be flexibility and room for surprises, allowing the students' work to take various paths.

When the story is finished, the adult retells the story using the action-symbol map, summarizing from the beginning and allowing the children to correct any "errors" in the details. Following immediately, the children draw their favourite scene from their class-created story. This drawing activity provides each child with further opportunity to make the story his or her own. Later on, the children can create their own individual story.

Preparation for class work with a story

Step 1. Choose a story.

a) Read the ten tales in the anthology following this chapter and decide which story you want to work with. All stories have been tested in the classroom and will give you results. There are five different categories, or tale types, to choose from, and I have provided you with a choice of stories in each, with the exception of the last tale type: The Helpers.

b) For your own use in the classroom, photocopy the tale you select and the accompanying materials:

- summary with action-symbols
- the template for an action-symbol map on storyboard (or magnetic board)
- guiding questions for creating a new story with the class
- notes

c) Read through the story a few times, not to memorize it but to understand what is happening and the sequence of events taking place.

Step 2. Create the story map and characters for the class-room demonstration.

    a) From the complete set of symbols on pages 228–243, select the symbols needed for the tale and photocopy them. It would be best to laminate them and cut them into single cards so that you can use them again for another class or another story.

    b) Arrange the symbols on the board in the classroom in the same sequence as you see it on the story's action-symbols map. If you have a magnetic board, put them on with magnets. If not, stick them on the board or on a wall with Fun Tak, or just tape them. You could attach the symbols with small binder clips onto a foam-core board or onto a card to make the story map portable. For my research project, I made copies of my symbols, glued them to flexible magnetic backing sheets bought at a craft-supply store, cut them out as individual symbols. Then, I placed the symbols on two portable magnetic boards, each 24 inches wide, and drew a trail around them so it resembled a path.

    c) Now, you need to make the story's characters for the hands-on demonstration, the re-enactment of the tale. If you have a magnetic board, use various magnets (different in colour and/or size) to represent them. Otherwise, use sticky notes in various colors. These are abstract indicators of the characters. You do not want them to look realistic!

The characters you will need are:

The hero/ine

In stories with two or three main characters, you might also differentiate between male and female with a different colour for each gender.

The helper

This is the magic animal or person the hero/ine meets along the way. I like to portray the helper in a shiny, metallic colour to indicate that this character is special.

The reward

Usually, this is the magical object the hero/ine receives from the helper or the object the hero/ine searches for. Select a small item in a different shape or colour to represent the reward.

The villain

Choose or make an unusual looking magnet or sticker with a shape or colour to indicate the nature of this character.

The adults in charge

These are the secondary characters who usually appear only at the beginning and the end of the story. They may be the parents, grandparents, or even a babysitter; that is, characters who are not part of the quest so are not essential in mapping the action, but they are nice to include. To represent the adults, you might pick some bigger magnets or sticky notes.

Step 3. Practice the characters' moves on the story's action-symbol map.

Once you have prepared the story map and the story's character icons, look at the "Summary with action-symbols" and practice moving the characters (the magnets or stickers) along the storyboard map. Use this step as a hands-on demonstration of the hero/ine's journey throughout the story. Move the magnet or sticker representing the hero/ine from one action-symbol to the next according to the story's summary. Because the other characters don't move as much, place them on or take them off the map as they enter or exit the story.

Go through the moves a few times on your own until you are comfortable doing them before you actually do this in front of the students. Then, cover the map or turn the storyboard to face a wall so that the children don't see the map until the time is right.

Steps to follow during the activity

When you have the map and the characters ready, and the chosen story, with its summary and guiding questions in front of you, you are set to go. Tell the children you are going to read them a fairy tale, but that this story has no pictures, so they can close their eyes and try to visualize the story in their mind like a movie. The reading will take you approximately 5 to 8 minutes. After the reading, you will summarize the story on the storyboard map. Then, you will guide the children so they can invent their very own story.

Step 1. Read the story from the sheet.

When you are finished, tell the children that you will now show them how the story went. Now is time to use the story's symbol map.

Step 2. Demonstrate the hero/ine's journey on the action-symbol map.

With the Summary sheet as a guide, move the story's characters from one action-symbol to the next as your re-telling progresses. When you are finished, tell the children that now it's their turn to invent their story. They will have to use their imagination and come up with their own ideas, which should be different from those in the fairy tale they have just heard.

Step 3. Ask the students guiding questions to help them create a new story.

Use the Guiding questions sheet for the tale you selected. As you ask the questions in sequence from the sheet, react to what the children tell you.

During the story's creation, your primary function is to listen to what the children suggest and guide them in the direction they want to go.

When the children come up with an answer to each question, tie the answer into a sentence for them. Then, ask the next question, and the children will suggest answers, and so on … like a game of ping-pong. Take a few suggestions from the students, but then you propose which idea to go with and get approval from the class (remember, it is their story). If a majority of the students do not agree with your proposed idea, ask for a few more suggestions, then let the children vote on them. But you do need to keep the story moving along so children don't lose their initial enthusiasm. Almost any idea the children will come up with will work in their story, but you can try to promote the more interesting ones.

Step 4. Summarize the children's story with the new characters and replay it on the action-symbol map.

Use the same magnets or sticky notes you prepared for the fairy tale to represent the new characters. If the new protagonist is of the opposite gender or if there are two, exchange the colour or add another magnet or a sticky note. Do the same thing to reflect the new family in the story. Ask the children to correct you if you make any errors as you progress through the summary of the class-created story. I found that when I confused the names of their characters or simply forgot what happened next in their story, the children always caught it immediately, and they let me know. This process of interactive story-creation may take about 20 to 30 minutes.

"During the story's creation, your primary function is to listen to what the children suggest and guide them in the direction they want to go."

Step 5. Have the children draw their favourite scene from their new story.

Supply the children with blank sheets of paper, pencils, and crayons. Ask them to draw the scene that they found the most interesting in their new story and to add details to the scene on their own. Allow about 15 minutes for this drawing phase of the activity, but if you can allow them more time, they will add more details to their pictures. Now check the time and you will see how much you have accomplished with the class in about 45 minutes!

Step 6.
a) **Move on to creating individual student's stories.**
b) **Choose a story from another tale-type category so the students can familiarize themselves with another story's pattern.**
c) **Show the students how they organized their story.**

At this point, show the children what they have done. Draw back the curtain and reveal the language components and the organization that they have accomplished with their own story. Point out that they created characters, a setting, a story's problem, and its resolution. After the students have accomplished the goal, let them know how smart they are and how they did it by showing them the steps they took.

Some practical concerns

The first ideas the students come up with are often the best because they are spontaneous reactions to what immediately preceded. When several students express different but interesting ideas, you may be able to combine some of them; if not, have the children vote for their choice. But do acknowledge all the ideas by mentioning that they are good and valid and could work in the story—which is true.

There should be no restrictions on the children's ideas. The children should have total freedom to invent. They should be the ones who control the story. However, if you feel uncomfortable with any of their suggestions, do bypass them or choose other ideas. It's important to be sensitive to the children's suggestions, because they are likely coming from the children's personal experiences.

- The story should start and end in a peaceful place, not in a cemetery, for instance.

- Do not make charts of ideas at the beginning of this story-creating activity—to do so prevents the children from reaching into their personal experiences as they go with the flow of the story. Their ideas will arise naturally during the story's creation when other children's ideas ignite their imagination. Children link ideas intuitively, logically, and spontaneously as they connect objects to actions.

- Do not use picture books or other visual material for this activity. The artistic interpretations of others would prevent the children from using their own imagination to visualize the story and its characters for themselves.

- Take care when students suggest using characters from video games in the stories. Using more than one video character in a story may prevent children from accessing their own imaginations. However, when the elements of video games can be used in a creative way as building blocks toward a new story, take advantage of the opportunity.

- For the adult who is the guide, the process involves listening, connecting, anticipating, and relating, but it can be a bit scary, like the feeling of walking into a dark tunnel. Problems may arise in the story, problems that you and the children have to solve on the spot to make the story work. But not to worry: that is when the action-symbol map comes into play. The map serves as a safety railing for you to hold on to so as not to get lost.

- It is better not to explain in depth what the action-symbols mean or to ask the children to memorize them. Let them absorb the symbols subconsciously so they don't really think about them while they are creating their story. Remember, the imagination resides on the intuitive right side of the brain.

- During this phase of the activity, as the children become engaged in creating their story, the atmosphere in the classroom may become quite charged and noisy. The noise and enthusiasm are outward manifestations that show that the children are truly involved. So, be prepared!

I have provided you with the ingredients and the recipe for how to use them. Now you have to make the meal, watch it, and stir it. It will require your full attention. You will be amazed how powerful children's imagination is and what kind of results you will get.

Teacher Materials

Anthology of Tales

The anthology provides ten stories from five categories of fairy tales. I selected and simplified them for my work with students in the classroom as I presented and evaluated my approach.

Teachers may copy each tale and the materials keyed to it for personal use in preparing to put my approach into practice with children in their classroom.

① **Summary and action-symbols**

The teacher may use the summary of each tale, describing the actions while demonstrating the hero/ine's journey on the map.

② **Template of the action-symbol map**

The teacher may replicate on a storyboard or magnetic board this template of the tale's action-symbol map for use with children in retelling the tale and then creating a new tale in the pattern of that tale type. (See page 163 for a description of storyboard.)

③ **Guiding Questions**

The teacher may use some or all of these to draw out the children's ideas for creating a class tale using a similar progression of actions.

④ **Notes**

The notes accompanying some tales are included to help teachers deal with unique difficulties that might be encountered with some classes.

⑤ **Complete set of action symbols** (pages 228 to 243)

These have been designed and illustrated by the author for use with Propp's actions, as discussed in Chapter 3.

Appendix A

Appendix B

Anthology of Fairy Tales

Tale type: The Children and the Ogre
① The Black Geese of Baba Yaga (Russian tale)
② Pedro and the Witch (Filipino tale)
③ Runaway Children (South African tale)

Tale type: Animal Bride
④ The Farmer's Boy and the Orange Cat (German tale)
⑤ The Mouse Bride (European tale)

Tale type: The Magic Objects
⑥ The Magic Soup Pot (Czech tale)
⑦ The Grinding Stones (Japanese tale)

Tale type: The Kind and the Unkind
⑧ The Golden Rain (American tale)
⑨ Three Gnomes in the Forest (German tale)

Tale type: The Helpers
⑩ Stretch, Swallow, and Stare (Czech tale)

Note: Each category appeals to children for different reasons, so choose whichever category and tale you prefer for your students. You may notice that the action-symbol maps of the tales in each category are very similar, if not identical.

**Tale type: The Children and the Ogre
#1 (Russian tale)**

The Black Geese of Baba Yaga

Adapted and retold by Veronika Martenova Charles © 2007

Once there was a man and woman who had two children, a girl and a boy. One day the parents had to go to the market so the mother said to her daughter, "Elena, while we're away, take care of your baby brother. But be careful! The black geese of Baba Yaga were seen flying over the village. So don't go outside. When we come back we'll bring you some sugar buns."

Elena knew about Baba Yaga. She was the terrible witch of the forest, who was eight feet tall and ate little children. After her parents left, Elena stayed in the house with her brother, but after a while she got bored. She saw her friends outside, so she took her brother, set him out on the grass and went to play with her friends, forgetting all about him.

After some time, she remembered and came back to look for him. But he was nowhere to be found. Then, far on the horizon, Elena saw the black geese. They were carrying something! She realized what must have happened: the black geese had taken her brother and were carrying him to Baba Yaga's hut. "I must go after him," she decided. And she ran toward the forest where Baba Yaga lived.

As she went over the fields she came to a pond. There, lying on the sand was a fish, gasping. "Elena," the fish called. "Please help me. I'm dying!" Now, Elena was in a hurry but she stopped, and put the fish back into the water. The fish popped her head out and said, "Because you helped me, I will help you. Pick up that shell which lies by your feet. If you're ever in danger, throw the shell over your shoulder and it will help you.

Elena couldn't see how the shell could possibly help her, but she didn't want to seem rude. So she picked up the shell and put it in her pocket. Then she ran on into the dark forest. Inside, trees grew so close together that not even a ray of light could shine through. Finally she came to a clearing … and there was Baba Yaga's hut.

It stood on two giant chicken feet and the black geese were sleeping on its roof. Elena crawled to the hut and peaked inside. There was water boiling on the stove and Baba Yaga was lying down, snoring.

Elena's brother was near her, sitting on the ground, playing with some bones. Elena crept in, grabbed her baby brother, and ran outside. But the black geese saw her. They honked and flapped their wings. It woke up Baba Yaga. She ran out and screamed, "Stop thief! Bring back my dinner!" And she ran after them.

Elena ran as fast as she could, but she carried her brother and he was heavy. Baba Yaga was getting closer and closer. When Elena looked back, she saw Baba Yaga within an arm's length. What could she do?

She remembered about the shell and she threw it over her shoulder. Instantly a big wide river appeared behind her. Baba Yaga could not go around it, so she waded into it. But the water was deep and Baba Yaga couldn't swim. It didn't take long before she drowned.

Elena got home with her brother just in time, as their parents returned and brought them some sugar buns.

Tale type: The Children and the Ogre – **The Black Geese of Baba Yaga**

Summary with action-symbols

 1.   Parents go to the market.

 2.   They say to Elena, "Take care of your baby brother and don't go outside."

 3.   Elena disobeys.

 8.   Black Geese of Baba Yaga steal Elena's brother.

 9./10.   Elena goes to find him.

 11.   She meets a fish that needs help.

TEST   12./13. Elena puts the fish back in the water.

 14.   The fish gives Elena a magic shell.

15.   Elena comes to Baba Yaga's hut.

Tale type: The Children and the Ogre – **The Black Geese of Baba Yaga**

16. She goes inside it,

 19. picks up her baby brother,

 20. and runs back home with him.

 21. Baba Yaga chases after them. She is fast.

SURVIVAL 22. Elena throws the magic shell over her shoulder.

 30. River appears and Baba Yaga drowns in it.

 31. When parents return, they bring Elena sugar buns.

Tale type: The Children and the Ogre – **The Black Geese of Baba Yaga**

Action-symbol map

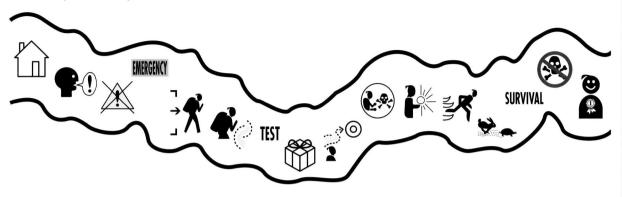

Guiding questions for creating a new tale

- Who should be the hero/ine? Is it a boy or a girl?
- What will be his/her name?
- Who else is at home? Who is in charge?
- The adults are going somewhere. Where are they going?
- What kind of responsibility do they give to the hero/ine? *(For instance: to look after some object, or someone, like a sibling or pet)*
- What warning do the adult/s give to the hero?
- Is there a villain? Who is he/she/it?
- What happens after the adult/s leave?
- How does the hero/ine react to the emergency?
- What does the landscape look like through which the hero/ine travels? Describe.
- Who does the hero/ine meet? (*The best is a magic animal, but it could be magical person or a talking object.*)
- The animal is in some kind of distress, and needs help. What kind of trouble?
- What does the hero/ine do to help?
- How does the animal respond and reward the hero/ine?
- What happens next?

Tale type: The Children and the Ogre – **The Black Geese of Baba Yaga**

- The hero/ine reaches the place of her/his search. What does the place look like?
- Who is inside? Is the villain inside? If he is there, what is he doing?
- What happens next? *(React to the specific answers.)*
- When the villain chases after the hero/ine, what does she/he do to survive? What happens when she/he does it and what happens to the villain? Describe.
- What do the adults bring to the hero/ine when they return back home?

Notes

- If, for instance, the magic animal gives the hero/ine a reward object (such as a ring or a coin) that makes wishes come true, the wish cannot bring the object of the hero's search back! There would then be no journey and the story would be over.
- If the villain is not established at the beginning of the created story by the children and the adult who guides them, the hero/ine may follow clues (let the children invent some), or be directed to the object by the magical animal the hero/ine encounters along the way. The villain should not steal the hero/ine. The structure map supplied would not be able to guide the new story's creation. A different map configuration is needed for that type of plot. On the other hand, if such a situation were to arise, you might just let it ride and see how the children resolve it themselves!
- The children may bypass or add to the actions in the story as represented by the symbols. The map is meant to guide and help reframe the story and also free the children's imagination. It does not have to be rigidly followed.

Tale type: The Children and the Ogre – **The Black Geese of Baba Yaga**

Tale type: The Children and the Ogre
#2 (Filipino tale)

Pedro and the Witch

Pedro lived with his mother and father by the seashore. One morning the parents went to look for food and they said to Pedro: "While we are gone, stay in the house. Don't open the door! Boroka, the witch, could come and eat you alive! We will be back by the evening."

But the evening came and the parents did not return. Pedro was hungry and could not sleep. In the middle of the night he heard tapping on the door. "That must be my parents," he thought and he rushed to greet them. But when he opened the door, he saw it was not his parents but the witch Boroka. She had wings like a bird, feet like a horse, and a head like a woman. She grabbed Pedro and carried him to her home in the mountains.

Pedro was not afraid of the witch Boroka and did what she told him, so she made him her housekeeper. "Don't ever try to run away!" the witch told Pedro. "I can easily catch you and then YOU will be my dinner."

Whenever the witch was away, hunting for people, Pedro would amuse himself, riding on the back of the horse that would often come to see him. The two became friends.

One day, the witch decided to have Pedro for dinner after all. She left the house and went to gather some herbs and berries for the dinner preparation. While she was gone, the horse came and told Pedro of the danger. It gave him two scarves, one red and the other one white. Then the horse told Pedro to jump on its back and it started to run. Not long afterward, Pedro noticed the witch Boroka was pursuing them. "Drop the red scarf!" the horse told Pedro. Pedro did as he was told and saw the red scarf change into a large fire. When the witch flew over, it burned her wings off. Still, even on the ground, the witch Boroka was faster than the horse. She was almost on their backs, when the horse commanded: "Drop the white one!" Pedro dropped the white scarf. It became a wide sea and Boroka could not go any further. Pedro was now safe and he returned home. He was glad to find his parents were back and they all were happy to see each other again.

Summary with action-symbols

 1. Parents go to look for food.

 2. They say to Pedro, "Don't open the door!"

 3. Pedro disobeys.

 8. The witch Boroka kidnaps Pedro.

15. She takes him to her home in the mountains

Tale type: The Children and the Ogre – **Pedro and the Witch**

16.   and makes Pedro her housekeeper.

 11.   Pedro meets a horse.

TEST 12./13. They become friends and Pedro takes the horse for rides.

 14.   The horse gives Pedro red and white scarves.

 20.   Pedro runs away from Boroka's place on the horse.

 21.   The witch Boroka flies after them.

SURVIVAL 22.   Pedro drops the scarves.

 30.   Boroka burns her wings and a wide sea stops her from going further.

 1a.   Pedro gets home and reunites with his parents.

Tale type: The Children and the Ogre – **Pedro and the Witch**

Action-symbol map

Guiding questions for creating a new tale

- Who will be the main character? What will be his/her name?
- Where does he/she live? With whom?
- Where do the adults go?
- What do they warn the hero/ine not to do? Why?
- Who is the villain?
- What happens after the adults leave? *(The hero/ine disobeys the warning.)*
- When the villain appears, what does he/she/it look like?
- Where does the villain take the hero/ine? Describe it.
- What job does the hero/ine have to do for the villain?
- Whom does the hero/ine meet in the villain's place? *(Best is a magic animal.)*
- How does the hero/ine befriend that "someone" in the villain's place?
- What does the hero/ine do for his new friend? What do they do together?
- How does the hero/ine find out he/she is in danger?
- What magic gift does he/she receive from that friend?
- What does he do then?
- How does the hero/ine use the magic gift to save him/herself?
- What happens when the hero/ine uses the magic gift?

Tale type: The Children and the Ogre – **Pedro and the Witch**

- What happens to the villain?
- What happens to the hero/ine's friend? How does the story end?

Notes

- If, for instance, the magical animal gives the hero/ine a reward object (such as a ring or a coin) that makes wishes come true, the wish cannot bring the object of the hero's search back! There would then be no journey and the story would be over.
- If the villain is not established at the beginning of the created story by the children and the adult who guides them, the hero/ine may follow clues (let the children invent some), or be directed to the object by the magical animal the hero/ine encounters along the way. The villain should not steal the hero/ine. The structure map supplied would not be able to guide the new story's creation. A different map configuration is needed for that type of plot. On the other hand, if such a situation were to arise, you might just let it ride and see how the children resolve it themselves!
- The children may bypass or add to the actions in the story as represented by the symbols. The map is meant to guide and help reframe the story and also free the children's imagination. It does not have to be rigidly followed.

Tale type: The Children and the Ogre – **Pedro and the Witch**

**Tale type: The Children and the Ogre
#3 (South African Tale)**

Runaway Children

Adapted by Veronika Martenova Charles from
Judy Sierra's version

Once there was a man in the village who had two small daughters. One morning the man told his daughters: "Go and bring some water!" The girls took a big clay pot and went down to the river. Along the way the younger girl stumbled, let go of the pot and it fell down and broke. "Look what you have done!" said her sister. "Now we're going to be punished," she cried. "We could hide somewhere for a while so our father can't find us," they said to each other and they walked away from the village.

As they walked through the woods, they came upon a baby bird lying helplessly on the ground. "Look," said the younger sister, "the bird must have fallen from its nest." So the older sister climbed up the tree and put the bird back into its home. Then they continued walking until it got dark, when they came upon a house in the woods. They knocked on the door and a woman answered. "Come inside," she said. "You can spend the night here." The sisters were glad not to have to sleep under the open sky, so they gladly accepted the woman's invitation.

They lay down but they could hear the sound of metal rubbing against the rock and the woman's voice singing: "Rock is smooth, rock is hard, and it makes my axe real sharp." The girls were frightened and cried out.

"What is the matter?" asked the woman. "Why aren't you asleep?" "We can't sleep," the girls answered. "It's too hot inside." The woman opened the window. "Now go to sleep," she said.

But in a little while, the younger sister started coughing. "What's the matter now?" the woman asked her. "Can I have a drink of water?" the girl asked the woman. The woman brought the girl a cup of water but by now she was becoming tired herself. She lay down and in few moments she started snoring. The sisters crawled out of the bed, leaving two rocks under the blanket in their place and ran away.

When the woman awoke from her sleep, she picked up her axe and swung it on the two bumps in the bed. "Clang, clang!" the axe made a sound as it hit the rocks. The woman screamed in anger. She ran out and set after the girls. She was fast and knew her way in the woods. Soon the sisters could hear her behind them and saw a cloud of dust rising from the ground.

To save themselves, the girls climbed up a tall tree and sat there, still and quiet. But the woman could smell them and stopped at the base the tree. "I know you are up there!" she called. She swung her axe into the tree trunk. "Chop, chop," the tree began to lean over. Then, a bird flew over and sang: "Wood chips make the tree trunk whole, make the tree stand straight and tall!" It was the mother of the baby bird that the girls saved the day before. It flew over to help them, returning the favour. Now, no matter how hard the woman tried to chop the tree down, the tree would always straighten up again.

Tale type: The Children and the Ogre – **Runaway Children**

From the treetop, the sisters could see a man and his dogs in the distance. They began shouting and waving at him. It was their father! He was searching for them. The dogs ran to the base of the tree, jumped on the woman and tore her to pieces. Then the father came and was happy to see his daughters. He forgave them for breaking the clay pot and they all returned back to the village.

Summary with action-symbols

	1.	A man has two daughters.
	2.	He asks them to bring a pot of water.
	8.	The girls break the pot. They are afraid that they'll be punished.
	9./10.	The girls run away to hide.
	11.	They find a baby bird on the ground …
	12./13.	And put it back into its nest.

Tale type: The Children and the Ogre – **Runaway Children**

15. The girls come to a house in the woods.

 16. A witch lives there and the girls have to outsmart her.

 20. The girls run away.

 21. The witch runs after the girls.

SURVIVAL 22. The mother of the baby bird saves the girls.

 30. The witch is killed by the dogs.

🏠 1a. Father forgives the girls for breaking the pot.

Action-symbol map

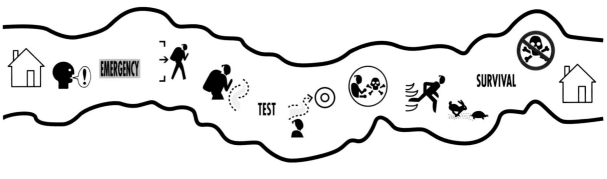

Tale type: The Children and the Ogre – **Runaway Children**

Guiding questions for creating a new tale

- Who will be the main character(s)?
- Who is/are the adult/s in the family?
- Where do they live?
- Why did the children run away? What did they do?
- Where are they running to? Describe the landscape or setting.
- Whom do they meet along the way? *(Some animal is the best.)*
- What happened to it? How do the children help? *(At this point, the students should be told that the animal will help the heroes later on in the story.)*
- What kind of a place do the children come to?
- Who is the villain that lives there?
- What does the villain tell the children? Describe their conversation.
- How do the children discover that they are in danger?
- How do they distract and trick the villain? Describe it.
- How do the children get away?
- What happens when the villain discovers the children are gone?
- What do the children do when the villain is chasing them?
- What happens when the villain is about to catch them? Who comes to their rescue?
- How does the magical animal help the children survive?
- How is the villain stopped so that he/she cannot do them any harm?
- What happens after the children return back home?

Note

The assisted animal, or whoever it is that the hero meets along the way, will be the one who will help the hero(es) later to survive.

Tale type: The Children and the Ogre – **Runaway Children**

Tale type: Animal Bride
#4 (German Tale)

The Farmer's Boy and the Orange Cat

Adapted and retold by Veronika Martenova Charles © 2007

Once there was a farmer who had three sons. The two older ones were strong and clever but the youngest one was small and did not talk much. So everyone just called him Dummling. The father was getting old and began to think of his end. One day he called his sons and said, "Go out into the world and bring me back a horse. Whoever brings the finest of horses will get the farm."

Then he took three feathers, blew them into the air, and said to his sons, "Follow the flight of the feathers." One feather flew to the east, the second flew to the west, and the third one flew straight ahead, but not very far. So, one son went to the left and another went to the right. But before they left, they said to Dummling, "You might as well stay home because you'll never get a horse for as long as you live." So Dummling went straight ahead and after a while he sat down on the ground and was sad.

As he sat there, he noticed a trap door in the ground, right next to the feather. He lifted the door and saw stairs going deep into the ground. He climbed down and walked through another door. There was a landscape just like the one above the ground. Dummling walked until he was tired, then he lay down and fell asleep. When he awoke, he saw a little orange cat staring at him.

"I know what you want," said the cat. "You're looking for a horse. If you come and work for me for one year, I will get you that horse." So Dummling went with the cat to her house. She gave him a silver axe and asked him to chop some wood. She gave him a silver hammer and nails and asked him to build her a little cottage. And so it went. When the year was over, Dummling asked the cat, "Can I have the horse?"

The cat told him, "You can see him, but you can't have him yet." She led him to the stable and there he was: the most beautiful horse Dummling had ever seen. The cat said, "Go home and in three days I will come and bring the horse to you." Then the cat showed him the way back up to the farm.

When Dummling got home, his brothers were already there. Each of them had brought back a horse. "So, where is your horse?" they asked Dummling.

"It's going to be delivered," Dummling answered.

But they laughed and said, "Yeah, sure … Where would you find a horse? Of course you wouldn't get one." And they did not let him even eat with them or sleep in the house. So Dummling had to stay in the barn.

Three days passed and a carriage arrived at the farm. A girl with orange hair just like the cat's stepped out of the carriage. She asked to see Dummling. The brothers answered, "You don't want to talk to him." But the girl insisted, so they brought him to her.

Then she asked to see the horses that the brothers had brought. One of their horses was blind and the other one was lame. The girl brought forward the horse that she had for Dummling. Everyone could see that this was the most magnificent horse.

The farmer said, "Dummling, the farm is now yours." But the girl said, "You can keep the farm as I have a house and a cottage your son built for me. And that's where we are going." Then she and Dummling climbed into the carriage and they rode off.

Summary with action-symbols

 1.   A farmer has three sons. The youngest is called Dummling.

 8a.   The farmer asks his sons to bring him a horse.

 x.   The father blows three feathers to show them which way to go.

 9./10. Dummling goes underground.

 11.   He meets an orange cat that offers to help him to get the horse.

 12./13. Dummling works for the cat.

Tale type: Animal Bride – **The Farmer's Boy and the Orange Cat**

20a. He goes back home with the cat's promise that the horse will be delivered.

1a. Dummling's brothers are home with the horses they brought.

23. The brothers make fun of Dummling and bully him.

25./26. Dummling copes and patiently waits for the horse.

19. The cat, now transformed into a girl, delivers the horse to Dummling.

27. Dummling has the best horse, inherits his father's farm, and finds love with the cat-girl.

Action-symbol map

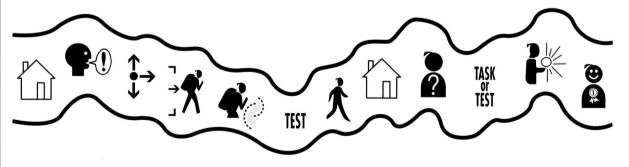

Tale type: Animal Bride – **The Farmer's Boy and the Orange Cat**

Guiding questions for creating a new tale

- What will be the name of the youngest son?
- What is the father's job?
- What does the father ask his sons to bring him?
- How does the father send his sons on the journey?
- What is the ritual?
- Where does it lead the hero?
- Describe the setting and what happens.
- Who does the hero meet there? How? *(The best is a magical animal.)*
- What kind of work does the hero have to do for …? Describe it.
- How long does the hero work there?
- What happens after the work is done?
- When does the hero get his reward? Does he get to see it? Where?
- Describe what happens.
- What happens when the hero returns home?
- What did the brothers bring from their journeys? Describe.
- What is the father's reaction? What does he say? Describe it.
- What happens to the magical animal?
- What happens to the brothers?
- How does the story end?

Note

The animal transformation into a girl may not happen as children seem uninterested in the generic happy endings of the tales consisting of a "boy/girl union, marriage" and "happily ever after." Instead, what seems to matter to the children is that justice is done in the story.

Tale type: Animal Bride – **The Farmer's Boy and the Orange Cat**

The Mouse Bride

Adapted and retold by Veronika Martenova Charles © 2007

Once an old king called his three sons to him and said, "I want you to go into the world and bring me the best hunting dog. Whoever brings the best dog will be king." "Where should we go to look for it?" asked the oldest son. "Make a bow and shoot an arrow. Then, follow its direction." their father replied.

The eldest son shot first and then went east. The second son's arrow flew west and so he followed it. The youngest son's arrow got stuck in the pile of firewood. Ivan, that was the youngest son's name, moved the wood to get the arrow and found to his surprise there was a small metal gate underneath. He lifted it and saw a tunnel, leading underground. Ivan entered and after a while came to a small room. It was empty, but there was food on a table and fire in a stove. A small mouse sat on the table. "Welcome!" she greeted Ivan. "Why do you look so sad? Eat if you're hungry. Stay if you're tired," she said.

"I don't need to eat or rest. I have another problem," Ivan told her. "I have to bring the best hunting dog to my father. If I come back empty-handed, everyone will laugh."

"Don't worry," said the mouse. "If you stay the night here with me, I will help you." Ivan stayed and in the morning the mouse gave him a small egg. "Don't open it until you get home," she said.

Ivan took the egg and fearfully went back home. His brothers returned before him and there were all kinds of dogs in the courtyard. The two older brothers presented their dogs to their father. "Let's see what you brought," said the father to his youngest son. Ivan handed him the egg and the father shook his head. Out of the egg popped a little green dog that barked, and ran ahead of all the others. Then the dog jumped back into the egg. "This is the best dog I have ever seen," said the king. The brothers didn't say much but later convinced their father that it must be some kind of a mistake and he should give them a second try. "Now go out, find yourself a bride and bring her here. Then, I will announce who will be king," the father said to his sons.

Again, the sons left for the road. Ivan went slowly, his head heavy with worry. He looked forward to seeing the little mouse, yet he doubted she would be able to help him this time. "Why are you so sad?" asked the mouse when Ivan came back to see her. "My father asked us to bring home our brides. What will I do?" Ivan said. "Why don't you bring me?" asked the mouse. "Who ever heard of a man having a mouse for a bride?" Ivan wondered. "Well, you couldn't be any worse off than you are now. If you like me, take me along," the mouse said. So Ivan agreed.

When they arrived at the palace, his brothers had already introduced their brides to their father. "Where is your bride?" the brothers asked Ivan. "She is standing beside me," Ivan told them and pointed to the mouse. "Guards!" called the brothers. "Come and kill the pest!" Ivan quickly picked up the mouse and held her against

Tale type: Animal Bride – **The Mouse Bride**

his body. "No!" he shouted. "She is my friend." Instantly, the mouse changed into a lovely young woman. She turned to Ivan and said, "You were not ashamed to bring me as your bride when I was a mouse. I hope you won't desert me now when I am human!" The father pronounced Ivan the future king and from then on Ivan and his bride lived happily for a long time.

Summary with action-symbols

	1.	A king has three sons.
	8a.	He asks them to bring the best hunting dog.
	x.	The sons shoot arrows to see which direction to go.
	9./10.	Ivan goes through a tunnel under ground.
	11.	He enters a room and finds a mouse there.
TEST	12./13.	The mouse offers to help Ivan if he stays the night with her.

Tale type: Animal Bride – **The Mouse Bride**

19. The mouse gives Ivan a magical egg with a dog inside it.

 20a. Ivan goes back home.

 1a. His brothers are there already with their dogs.

 23. The brothers question Ivan's accomplishment and demand a second try.

8a. Repeat. Father asks his sons to bring home brides. Note: In the second journey, the last symbol, number 23, is replaced with symbol 27.

27. When the mouse transforms into a girl, Ivan's victory is finally recognized. Ivan becomes the next king and marries the mouse-girl.

Action-symbol map

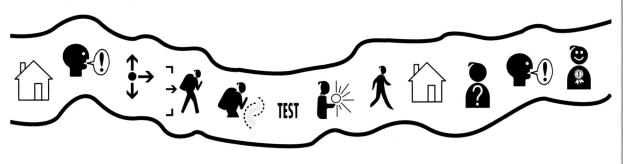

Tale type: Animal Bride – **The Mouse Bride**

Guiding questions for creating a new tale

- What will be the name of the youngest son?
- What is the father's job?
- What does the father ask his sons to bring him?
- How does the father send his sons on the journey?
- What is the ritual?
- Where does it lead the hero?
- Describe the setting and what happens.
- Who does the hero meet there? Describe what happens and what they talk about. *(The best is a magical animal.)*
- What kind of work, task or test does the hero have to do for the magical animal? Describe it.
- What happens after the work is done? What is his reward? What does it look like?
- What happens when the hero returns home?
- What did the brothers bring from their journeys? Describe what they brought home.
- What is the father's reaction to the presents he receives? What does he say?
- How do the older brothers react? What do they say to their father?
- What is the father's next request?
- *Repeat, starting from the journey to the magical animal place.*
- What happens to the magical animal?
- What happens to the brothers?
- How does the story end?

**Tale type: The Magical Objects
#6 (Czech tale)**

The Magic Soup Pot

Adapted and retold by Veronika Martenova Charles © 2007

In a village lived a poor man whose only possessions were a house with a leaky roof and a goat. Once he had nothing left to eat at home so he decided to go to the town nearby and sell his goat in the market.

As he walked through the woods he felt hot and tired so he sat down in the shade to rest. It was exactly noon. Suddenly an old woman appeared, dressed in rags like a beggar.

"Good day!" she said. "Where are you going?" The man told her he was off to sell his goat as he had nothing left to eat at home.

"I can help you," the woman said. She pulled out a rusty pot from her bag. "I can trade you this pot for your goat. You will not regret it. All you have to do is to say to it, 'Cook, pot! Cook!' and it will cook a delicious soup for you. When you have enough, just say to it, 'Stop, pot! Stop!' and it will stop cooking. But don't tell anyone about it!"

So the man traded his goat for the pot and the woman vanished as suddenly as she had appeared. When the man returned home he put the pot on the table and said to it, "Cook, pot! Cook." And before you could count to ten, the pot was full of soup. "Stop, pot! Stop!" the man commanded and it stopped filling. Then he ate his soup and was happy, as he would never be hungry again.

A few days later, a neighbour was passing by his house. Through the window she smelled the delicious soup. "How come," she wondered, "this poor man can afford such a delicious meal?" She knocked on the door and invited herself in. The man shared his soup with her as she pried and asked him questions. Finally the man told her about the magic pot. "And all you have to do is to say, 'Cook, pot! Cook!' Right?" she said, just to make sure. She couldn't get the pot out of her mind.

Next time the man went out for a walk, the neighbour came in with her own rusty pot and secretly exchanged it for the magic one. She took it home and said to it, "Cook, pot! Cook." And sure enough the soup began bubbling inside. It grew so fast, that the pot was nearly full. "I must get a plate and spoon," she said. When she returned, the soup was already pouring over the table and onto the floor. She didn't know how to stop it, so she put the plate on top of the pot. But it fell off and the soup just kept flowing. Soon her whole house was full of soup. To save herself from drowning, the neighbour climbed on the roof.

"Help!" she called as the soup was pouring out of the door and onto the road like a river. Just then the poor man was coming back to his house. He realized what had happened. "Please, make the pot stop!" the neighbour begged the man. So the man called out, "Stop, pot! Stop." And the river of soup stopped rising.

It took the neighbour weeks of hard work to clean up her house, all slimy from the soup. As for the man, he got his pot back and was never hungry again.

Tale type: The Magical Objects – **The Magic Soup Pot**

Summary with action-symbols

 1.   In the village lives a poor man.

 8a.   The man needs to get food.

 9./10.   He goes to the market to sell his goat.

 11.   Along the way the man meets an old woman.

TEST   12./13. She offers to trade him a rusty pot for his goat.

 14.   The man receives a magic soup pot and the instructions.

 20a.   The man returns home.

 31.   He uses the magic pot and it makes a delicious soup.

 4.   Nosy neighbour asks questions about the soup.

Tale type: The Magical Objects – **The Magic Soup Pot**

5. She finds out about the magic soup pot and steals it.

 8. The neighbour doesn't know how to stop the magic pot and her house gets flooded with soup.

 25./26. The man stops the magic pot.

 30. The neighbour has to clean up her house from the soup.

Action-symbol map

Guiding questions for creating a new tale

- Who will be the main character—a boy, a girl, a man or a woman?
- What will be the hero/ine's name?
- Who does the hero/ine live with?
- What does the hero/ine need?
- Which of his/her possessions is the hero/ine going to sell so he can buy it?
- Where does the hero/ine go to sell it?
- Whom does the hero/ine meet along the way?
- What's unusual about this person *(or an animal)*? What does he/she/it look like?
- What kind of an object does that person offer to trade in for the hero/ine's possession?
- What are the instructions for using the object?
- What happens after that?
- Who gets jealous?
- How does the person find out about the magic object and how to make it work?
- How does the person get the magic object from the hero/ine? Describe.
- What happens after the person gets the magic object?
- What sort of emergency does the object create for the person?
- How does the hero/ine find out that his/her magic object was stolen?
- How does the hero/ine stop the emergency the object created?
- How does the person who stole the object get punished?
- Does the hero/ine get his magic object back? How does the story end?

The Grinding Stones

In a village there were two brothers. The older brother lived in a big house and was stingy and unpleasant, while the younger one who lived in a rented little hut, was kind and nice. Once, the day before a New Year's celebration, the younger brother had nothing to eat at home. He went to borrow some rice from his older brother. "What is this?" yelled the older brother. "How can you be so stupid not to have any rice for the New Year celebration? Go away and leave me alone." And he slammed the door in his brother's face.

The younger brother went back home, not knowing what to do. He was crossing a stream when he saw an old man who was picking wood. "Where are you going?" asked the old man. "Nowhere in particular. Tomorrow is the New Year celebration and I don't have even one grain of rice at home," the young man answered. "Well, that's too bad. I will give you this little dumpling," the old man said. "Go over to the temple in the forest. Behind it there is a hole in the ground and kobito, little people, live there. They will ask you for the dumpling and offer you all kinds of things for it, but tell them all you want are the grinding stones. Then at home, turn the stones to the right and anything you want will come out. If you turn them to the left, they will stop."

The younger brother thanked the old man and went to the temple in the forest as he had been told. He found the hole and climbed into it. There he saw a large number of kobito, little people. They were making lots of noise as they tried to climb up on stalks of grass but were falling off. The young man picked them up to help them. "Oh, what a huge and strong man you are," the kobito said in awe. Then they noticed the dumpling that he carried and pleaded, "Please let us have it!" And they offered him some gold. "All I want for it are the grinding stones," said the younger brother as instructed. Though not happy about it, the kobito handed them over.

When the younger brother returned home, his wife impatiently asked, "Where have you been? Did you get rice from your brother?"

"Don't worry," the young man answered. He put the stones on the straw mat. "Make rice, make rice," he said, turning them to the right. Rice came pouring out in a stream. Then he asked for salted fish and other things necessary for the New Year feast. "Since we are now so rich, let's make us a new house." He turned the stones and a mansion appeared. He invited all his neighbours and relatives to come to the feast. Everyone was surprised, especially the older brother. At the feast, the younger brother decided to make some sweet cakes to give out as presents, so he went into the adjoining room and said, "Make sweets, make sweets," and turned the stones. The older brother spied on him and saw how it was done.

When the feast was over and the younger brother went to bed, the older brother crept into the house and stole the grinding stones. He also took some leftover sweets and then fled to the seashore. Then he got into his boat to get far from the village. After some time, he got hungry and ate the stolen sweets but then was overcome by a desire for some salt. He turned the stones and said, "Make salt, make salt." Right away, salt began to pour out and it would not stop. The older brother didn't know how to stop it. The salt kept rising; it sank the boat, and the brother sank with it. Now the stones are on the bottom of the ocean still grinding the salt, and that is why the sea is salty.

Summary with action-symbols

 1.   There are two brothers. The older one is rich, the younger one is poor.

 8a.   The younger brother needs rice for a New Year's celebration.

 9./10.   The younger brother goes to borrow rice from his brother but he doesn't succeed.

 11.   He meets an old man who gives him a dumpling and instructs him how to get grinding stones and how to use them.

Tale type: The Magical Objects – **The Grinding Stones**

TEST 12./13. The younger brother does exactly as he is told.

 14. He trades a dumpling from the old man for the grinding stones.

 20a. He returns home.

 31. He turns the stones and they give him everything he wants.

 4. His older brother spies on him

INFORMATION 5. and steals the grinding stones.

EMERGENCY 8. The older brother flees on his boat. He asks the stones to make him some salt but doesn't know how to stop the stones from grinding.

 30. The salt sinks the boat with the older brother.

Tale type: The Magical Objects – **The Grinding Stones**

Action-symbol map

Guiding questions for creating a new tale

- Who will be the main character—a boy, a girl, a man or a woman?
- What will be the hero/ine's name?
- Where does the hero/ine live? In the city? In the country?
- What does the hero/ine or someone in his/her family need?
- How will the hero/ine try to get it?
- Whom does the hero/ine meet along the way?
- What's unusual about this person or an animal? What does he or it look like? Describe.
- What do they say to each other? Describe their conversation.
- How does that magical person or an animal offer to help the hero/ine? What does the hero/ine have to do to get what he/she needs?
- What is the hero/ine supposed to do with the object he/she receives? Are there any special instructions to make the object work and to stop?
- What happens when the hero/ine returns home?
- Who gets jealous?
- How does that person find out about the magic object and how to make it work?
- How does that person steal the magic object? Describe.
- What happens after the person gets the magic object?

Tale type: The Magical Objects – **The Grinding Stones**

- What sort of emergency/disaster does the magic object create for the person?
- How does the hero/ine find out his/her magic object was stolen?
- How does the hero/ine stop the emergency?
- How does the person who stole the object get punished?
- Does the hero/ine get the magic object back? How does the story end?

Tale type: The Magical Objects – **The Grinding Stones**

Tale type: The Kind and the Unkind
#8 (American tale)

The Golden Rain

Once there was a woman who had two daughters. The girls were born twins, but they were very different from each other. One was ugly and lazy and the other one was pretty and helpful. Their mother favoured the ugly one and made a pet of her. The pretty, helpful girl was made to do all the work around the place. She had to serve meals to her mother and twin sister and to pick things up after them in the house.

One day she was told to bring some water from the lake. When the girl bent down to fill the bucket with water, she slipped and fell into the lake. She fell down and down through the water and on down past the water. When she opened her eyes again, she found herself in a green field, with blooming wild flowers and singing birds. Falling through the water and landing in such a place put her in such a state of shock that she just sat there until she calmed down. Then, she got up and began walking across the field.

First she came to a little house with some bread baking in the oven. The bread said to her, "Please take me out of this oven or I'll burn. Hurry!" The girl took the bread out of the hot oven and set it to cool. The bread said to her, "Thank you. Put a piece of fresh bread in your pocket to eat while you're travelling."

Next she came to a walnut tree bending down to the ground with a heavy load of nuts. The walnut tree said to her, "Please shake my branches and make some of the nuts fall down so I won't break down." The girl shook off nuts until the branches rose up a bit. The walnut tree said, "Thank you. Take some nuts for your journey."

Last the girl came to a house where an old woman was working. "Please," the old woman said, "Come inside and cook me some dinner. I'm tired and can't do it myself."

The girl made a meal for the old woman and for herself, cleaned up the dishes, and shook up the feather blanket so that the old woman could rest easy. Weeks and months passed by and the girl went on living at the old woman's house, doing all the work, taking care of the garden, even sewing new clothes for the old woman. After some time, the girl got homesick and wanted to go back for a visit, even though she was treated there so badly.

"Since you served me so well, I will take you up there again," the old woman said and led the girl to a door. When it opened and the girl stood right beneath the doorway, a shower of gold came pouring down on her until she was completely covered with it. Suddenly the door closed and the girl found herself standing near her mother's house. She went inside and her mother and twin sister wondered how she got to be so covered with gold. The girl told them where she had been and what took place.

The twin sister wanted to have a shower of gold fall on her, too, so she went to the lake and jumped into it. It happened the same way with her, only she wouldn't help the things that begged her to. She walked right on

Tale type: The Kind and the Unkind – **The Golden Rain**

and let the bread burn to ashes, and she let the walnut tree break down under the heavy load of nuts. At the old woman's house she did very little to help and complained a lot. After a while, the old woman told her to leave. As the girl went out of the door, sticky paint came down, pouring all over her. It didn't come off no matter how hard she tried to wash it off. She had to live like that, all dirty and sticky for rest of her days.

Summary with action-symbols

 1. Mother has twin daughters and prefers the lazy one.

 2. She asks the other, helpful daughter to bring some water.

EMERGENCY 8. The girl falls into the lake and through the water to another place.

 9./10. The girl starts walking.

 11. She helps the bread and the tree, and then she meets an old woman.

Tale type: The Kind and the Unkind – **The Golden Rain**

TEST 12./13. The woman asks the girl to work for her.

 14. She rewards the girl with a shower of gold.

 20a. The girl goes back home.

 31. She is all covered in gold. Her mother and sister can't believe their eyes.

 1a. The lazy sister wants the same thing to happen to her, too.

The story is repeated (from symbol 8 onwards) with the lazy sister who acts differently—she jumps into the lake and does not help anyone. She gets rewarded with sticky paint poured all over her.

Note: In the second journey, the last symbol, number 31, is replaced with symbol 30.

 30a. She had to live all dirty and sticky for the rest of her life.

Tale type: The Kind and the Unkind – **The Golden Rain**

Action-symbol map

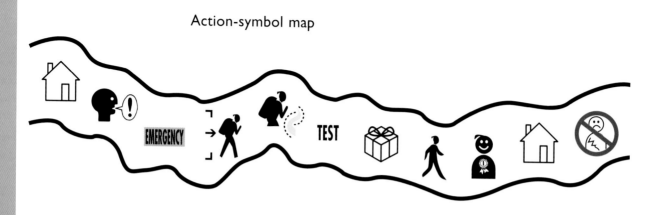

Guiding questions for creating a new tale

- Who will be the two main characters: two girls, two boys, or a boy and a girl?
- What will be the name of the kind character?
- What will be the name of the unkind character? (The name of the unkind sibling should not reflect names of the students as the character comes to an unpleasant end!)
- Who is the adult they live with?
- Why does the adult in charge prefer the unkind child? How does that show?
- What does the other, kind child have to do for the rest of the family?
- What difficult task is she/he asked to do?
- What happens? How does she/he get into the other, magic world?
- What does it look like in the other world? (Let the children describe the setting.)
- Who does the hero/ine meet there? (It could be a talking object or a magic animal or a person.)
- What is the hero/ine asked to do?
- How does the hero/ine react?

Tale type: The Kind and the Unkind – **The Golden Rain**

- How does the animal or object respond? Is the hero/ine rewarded? How?
- What happens next?
- What kind of a place does the hero/ine come to? Who lives in there?
- What is the hero/ine asked to do?
- Describe what she/he does there.
- How does she/he get rewarded for her work? Describe the magical reward.
- How does the family react when she/he returns back home?
- Repeat the journey with the other unkind character.

Notes

- When creating a story with the symbol maps of "Golden Rain" and "Three Gnomes in the Forest," you might recognize that the repeat of the second journey (the other protagonist) gets a bit boring for the children. Also, you might want to do just one test; I found that additional ones were too repetitive for the children. They did not appear to care about making three tests for the protagonist—one seemed to be sufficient.
- Take care when picking a name for the unkind character as he or she will be punished. The name should not reflect any names of the students.

Tale type: The Kind and the Unkind – **The Golden Rain**

Three Gnomes in the Forest

There was a man who had a wife and small daughter. Then his wife died and the man married a woman who also had a small daughter. And so it happened that the new wife did not like her stepdaughter and made life very hard for her.

Once, when it was winter and everything was covered with snow, the wife made a dress out of paper, called her stepdaughter, and said, "Now put on this dress, go to the forest, and bring me a basket of strawberries. I have a craving for them."

"How can I do that?" the girl said. "Strawberries don't grow in winter. And I will freeze in the paper dress."

"You have a nerve to talk to me like that!" said the stepmother. "Get going and don't show your face here until you bring the basket of strawberries." Then she gave her a little piece bread and said, "Here is your food for the day."

The girl put on the paper dress and went into the snow. When she reached the forest, she saw a little cottage, and three little gnomes were looking out of the window. The girl knocked on their door. "Come in," the gnomes called out. She entered and sat down near the fire to eat her bread. "Give us some bread too," asked the gnomes. "Gladly," replied the girl and divided the bread into pieces. "What are you doing in the forest?" the gnomes asked. "I'm looking for strawberries," she answered. "I can't go back until I have a basket full." After she finished eating, the gnomes asked her to sweep the snow away from the back door. Once she was outside, the gnomes began talking among themselves. "What should we give her for being so kind and sharing her bread with us?" asked one. "Each time she speaks, let's make a piece of gold fall out of her mouth. This will be our gift," said the other two gnomes.

Meanwhile, the girl swept the snow away from the back of the house. What do you think she found? There were lots of red ripe strawberries underneath. She filled the basket, thanked the little gnomes and rushed back home. As she entered the house and said, "Good evening," a piece of gold fell out of her mouth. Then she explained what had happened to her in the forest and with each word, a piece of gold fell out until the entire floor was covered with gold.

The stepsister was jealous and wanted the same thing to happen to her. She pleaded with her mother to let her go to look for strawberries, too, until her mother gave in. Then she put on a fur coat, took a big cake the mother baked for her, and headed straight for the cottage. The three gnomes were looking out of the window. She barged in uninvited, settled by the fire, and began to stuff herself with the cake. "Give us some," the little men asked. But she answered, "It's hardly enough for me. Get your own food." When she finished eating, the gnomes said to her, "Go outside and sweep the snow by the back door." The girl said, "Do it yourself! I'm not your

---

Tale type: The Kind and the Unkind – **Three Gnomes in the Forest**

servant." Then she went outside to get the strawberries and when she didn't find any, she went home in a bad mood. Meanwhile, the three gnomes began talking among themselves. "What should we give her for being so greedy and rude?" asked one. "Each time she says a word, let a toad jump out of her mouth. That will be our gift," said the other two gnomes.

When the girl came home and began telling her mother what happened, a toad jumped out of her mouth with every word she spoke. From then on, people wouldn't go near her. She had to live alone and soon died in misery.

Summary with action-symbols

1. A woman treats her stepdaughter badly but spoils her own child.

2. Woman tells her stepdaughter to bring strawberries in winter,

8. and not to come back without them. She gives her a paper dress.

9./10. The girl walks in the snow into the forest.

Tale type: The Kind and the Unkind – **Three Gnomes in the Forest**

11. She comes to a house of three gnomes.

TEST 12./13. The gnomes ask her for food and to sweep the snow. She does both.

14. The gnomes give her strawberries and gold, every time she speaks.

20a. The girl returns back home.

31. The stepsister is jealous of her good fortune.

1a. The stepsister wants the same thing to happen to her, too.

The story is repeated (from symbol 8 onwards) with the stepsister, who is rude to the three gnomes and refuses to help. She gets rewarded with a toad jumping out of her mouth, every time she talks.

30a. The stepsister had to live alone and died in misery.

Tale type: The Kind and the Unkind – **Three Gnomes in the Forest**

Action-symbol map

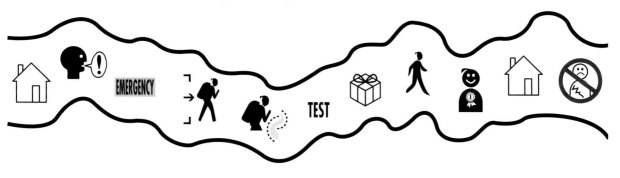

Guiding questions for creating a new tale

- Who will be the main character—a boy or a girl?
- What will be his/her name?
- Who will be the new adult in the house—a stepparent, aunt, babysitter?
- What is the name of his/her child they brought along to live with them? *(The name of this child should not reflect any names of the children in class as this character is portrayed as being nasty and comes to a bad end!)*
- How is the new adult's child being spoiled? How does it show?
- How does the new adult and his/her child make life hard for the hero/ine?
- What difficult thing is the hero/ine asked to bring?
- How does she/he set out on the journey? Does the new adult help her?
- Where is the hero/ine going? What does the landscape, cityscape look like? Describe it.
- Whom does she/he meet? Where? What does the place she/he/it lives in look like? Describe it.
- What is she/he asked to do? Does she do it? How is she/he rewarded?
- When she/he returns home, what is the reaction of the family?

Tale type: The Kind and the Unkind – **Three Gnomes in the Forest**

- What happens when the other child in the family wants the same thing to happen to her/him?
- How does the other character set out on the journey?
- Repeat the journey with the other "unkind" character.

Stretch, Swallow & Stare

Adapted from her own re-telling by Veronika Martenova Charles © 2007

Once, in the village, there was a man and a woman who had two children. The older one, a daughter, was called Kate and her brother was named Ira. Then the parents died, and Kate and Ira had to care for each other.

One day, some of the village children vanished without a trace. Ira's sister Kate was among them. "I've got to find my sister!" Ira thought. "She is the only family I have!" So Ira set out to look for Kate. He walked for a long time and entered a deep forest. "Where are you going?" he heard someone call. He looked around and saw a giant woman, taller than the tallest trees. "I'm looking for my sister Kate. And who are you?" Ira asked. The woman shrank herself in size. "They call me Stretch because I can make myself tall," the woman told Ira. "If you let me come with you, maybe I could help." So Ira asked Stretch to come along.

After a while they came to a village. They met a large woman with a body so round that she looked like a small mountain. "Who are you?" Ira asked. "They call me Swallow because I can eat a lot and make myself wide," the woman replied. After Ira told her about his sister, Swallow said, "If you let me come with you, maybe I could help." So Ira, Stretch, and Swallow continued on their way.

Fairy Tales in the Classroom

Soon they came to the mountains and met a woman with a blindfold over her eyes. "Who are you?" Ira asked. "How can you see with your eyes covered?" "They call me Stare," the woman answered. "My eyes are so strong that they burn through anything I look at. That's why I have to cover them," she said. Ira told Stare about his missing sister. "Just this morning, I saw some children in a castle not far away from here," Stare told him. "If you let me come with you, maybe I can help." Together they walked on.

Finally they reached the castle. They entered, and everywhere they looked they saw sleeping children. Ira searched for Kate among them. "Here she is!" he called, but he couldn't wake her. Suddenly, a wizard appeared. "I know why you're here," the wizard growled. "Let's play a little game. You guard your sister and I'll try to steal her away. If she is here when the sun comes up, I will let her go. If she is not, you'll pay with your lives." Then he was gone.

Ira sat down beside Kate. Stretch made herself long and wound herself around them. Swallow got wide and wedged herself in the doorway, while Stare took up guard by the window. Still, the wizard's power put them to sleep. At midnight, Ira woke up and saw that Kate was gone. He woke up his friends. "I see her!" said Stare. "She is inside a shell on the bottom of the sea." "I can take you there," offered Stretch. They climbed on her back and Stretch ran, taking a mile with each step. When they reached the sea, Swallow lay on the ground and began drinking it. Once the sea was dry, Stretch found

Tale type: The Helpers – **Stretch, Swallow & Stare**

the shell, took Kate out, and they rushed back to the castle. They got back just in time. The wizard was on his way. When he saw the girl was there, he screamed in anger. The wizard's rage set him on fire, and all that was left of him was a pile of ashes.

Now all the children woke up and Ira reunited with his sister. Stretch, Swallow, and Stare stayed with them, and then helped the other children to find their way home.

Summary with action-symbols

1. Ira lives with his older sister Kate.

8. One day Kate disappears.

9./10.   Ira goes to search for his sister Kate.

11. He meets Stretch, Swallow, and Stare, who join him.

15. They come to the wizard's castle where Kate and other children are held.

16. Ira and his friends confront the wizard.

Tale type: The Helpers – **Stretch, Swallow & Stare**

25./26. The wizard plays a game with them by giving them a task.

 30. The wizard loses and he self-destructs.

 19. The spell is broken and Kate and other children wake up.

 20a. Ira and Kate go back home.

 1a. Stretch, Swallow, and Stare take the other children home.

Action-symbol map

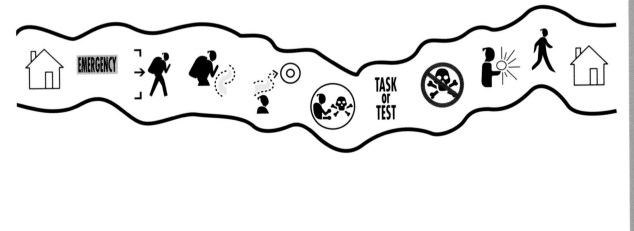

Tale type: The Helpers – **Stretch, Swallow & Stare**

Guiding questions for creating a new tale

* Who will be the hero/ine—a boy or a girl, a man or a woman?
* What will be his/her name?
* Where does the hero/ine live? In the town or in the country?
* What precious thing *(object, animal, or person)* was taken from the hero/ine?
* Who is the villain who took it? Why?
* Where does the hero/ine go to search for it? Describe the landscape, weather.
* Whom does the hero/ine meet? What is the unusual or magical ability that the person *(or an animal)* has? *(At this point, it is important to tell the students that the unusual ability will have to win the test or a contest with the villain later on in the story!)*
* What is that person's *(or animal's)* name? *(It should reflect his/her unusual quality.)*
* What will the hero/ine and the magical person talk about when they meet?
* How do they know where to go now, or that that they have arrived at the villain's place?
* What does the villain's place look like?
* How do they get inside and what happens when they meet the villain?
* What test is the hero/ine given to get the precious thing back from the villain?
* How does the magic ability of the person help the hero/ine to accomplish the task or the test? Describe what happens.
* What happens afterwards?
* What happens to the villain?
* How does the story end?

Tale type: The Helpers – **Stretch, Swallow & Stare**

Note

When inventing the helper with a magic power or a special ability, it is important to establish that, later in the story, the helper's special ability has to win the test or contest with the villain!

Master Set of Symbols

1. Parents leave or are absent from home

2. Request or warning to the hero/heroine

3.　　Hero/ine disregards the warning and villain appears

4.　　Villain asks question about the object, person he wants to get

INFORMATION

5.   Villain gets the information

6.   Villain tricks the hero, assumes a disguise

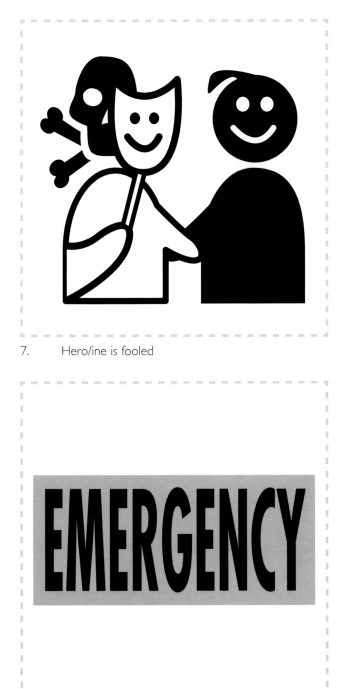

7.   Hero/ine is fooled

EMERGENCY

8.   Villain steals the object or abducts a person

8a.   Parent needs or desires to have something

9./10.   Hero/ine goes or is sent on journey to search
          for it and bring it back

11.   Hero/ine meets a magical animal or person

12./13. Hero/ine is tested for kindness and help.
        Hero/ine reacts

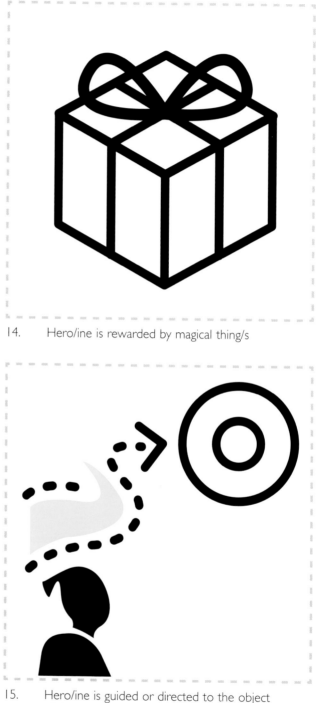

14.   Hero/ine is rewarded by magical thing/s

15.   Hero/ine is guided or directed to the object
        of the search

16.   Hero/ine confronts the villain

17.   Hero/ine is wounded

18. Villain is defeated

19. The object of the search is obtained and the spell is broken

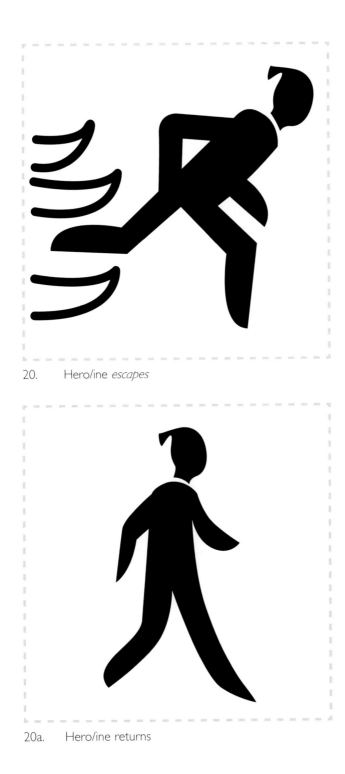

20.   Hero/ine *escapes*

20a.   Hero/ine returns

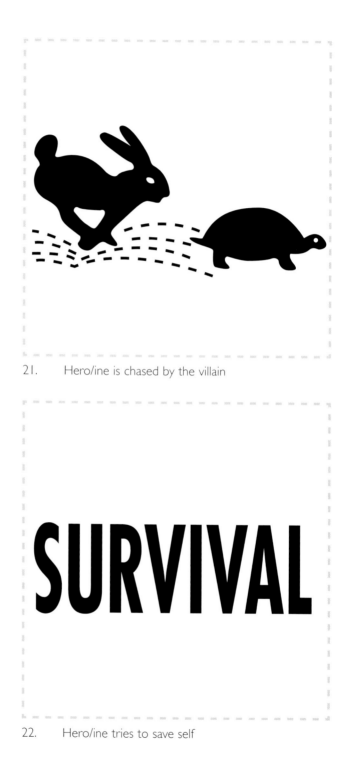

21.   Hero/ine is chased by the villain

SURVIVAL

22.   Hero/ine tries to save self

23.   Hero/ine arrives home unrecognized, unappreciated

24.   Someone else claims to be the hero/ine and claims
       the prize

TASK or TEST

25./26. Hero/ine undertakes test or task.
Test or task is accomplished

27. Hero/ine is recognized

28.   Villain is exposed

30.   Villain or impostor is punished

Additional symbols

30a.   Villain or impostor is punished

31.   Hero/ine is rewarded and/or is married

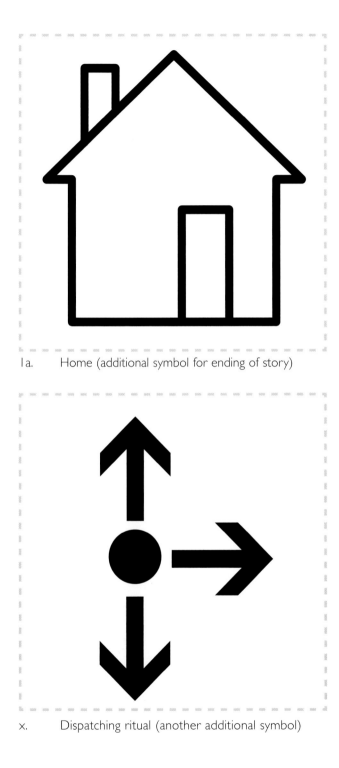

1a.   Home (additional symbol for ending of story)

x.   Dispatching ritual (another additional symbol)

Appendix A

The following are some examples of Rodari's games with fairy tales, described on pages 32–42 in his book *Grammar of Fantasy.*

1. Making mistakes in the story

The children are given a few words (five, for example) that suggest a fairy tale with which they are familiar. An additional word (the sixth) is, however, unexpected and has nothing to do with the fairy tale as the children know it. The children then react to that particular word and, in retelling the story, that word takes the tale in a different direction because it injects the "unexpected" into the tale. For instance, if Little Red Riding Hood meets a horse on the way to her grandmother's house, rides him, and gets to the house first before the wolf, it changes everything. For Rodari, the concern here is not whether the story arising from the introduction of the unexpected element will be any good or valid, but rather that the unexpected word ignites the imagination and sets things in motion so that the children will experience the pleasure and power of inventing.

2. Fairy tale reversed

The scenarios of the resulting stories may be altered: for example, Cinderella is the bad character and the stepmother and stepsisters are good; or Snow White encounters seven giants instead of seven dwarfs; and so on. The reversal often takes the story in a totally different direction.

3a. What happens if, during the tale, another motif is favoured?

The new story can take off from the recognition of the constructive impulse in the fairy tale. For instance, another motif in the story can be treated with preference and can be played out instead, thus recreating the tale.

3b. What happens after the fairy tale is finished?

The story can just continue although it had previously come to the end.

4. Fairy tale salad

By bringing another known fairy tale character into one well-known tale, new energy is injected into the tale. Mixing tales together will bring familiar characters into new and unexpected situations.

5. Recasting

In this game, a new fairy tale can arise from an old one. The game is more complex than the previous ones because it requires several steps. The first step is to reduce the fairy tale to its bare events and their internal relationships. For instance, Cinderella lives with her stepmother and stepsisters who go to a grand ball.

The second step is to convert those events to an abstract expression: A lives with B and C and D who go to an event F. Rodari calls the abstraction the "formula for forgetting the original tale." However, for me, it is difficult to imagine young children doing this and having fun. It's possible that something could be done with older children or by the teacher, because the process is time-consuming and requires higher analytical thought.

When a sufficient distance is created from the original tale, a new story can develop. The abstraction can be turned back into a concrete tale but set in a different place and played by different characters:

> Carlo is a stable boy at the estate of Count Cindertolis, father of William and Anne. It is vacation time, and the count and his children decide to take a journey around the world in their yacht.

In the two steps of the recasting game, the reduction and the abstraction are the preparation for the creation of the new story.

Appendix B

If you decide to work with tales other than the samples included, you may want to start by referencing the standard classification system developed by folklorists Antti Aarne and Stith Thompson, *The Types of the Folktale*, which can be found in most reference and university libraries. This system catalogues basic plots of tales spanning geographical areas from India to Ireland. Indo-European storytellers built their stories from these plots for generations. For stories from different parts of the world, other scholars have created similar types of indexes.

In the Aarne-Thompson classification index, the tales are arranged into categories called "tale types," and each is given a number and descriptive name (for instance, AT 327—The Children and the Ogre). Each type classification carries a brief description of the tale's plot and lists various geographic locations where the stories were found. The stories with similar plots are called "variants," which could be viewed as costumes of various materials, colours, and shapes being put on the skeleton of the tale type.

After you select the tale type you want to work with, locate the actual text of the story. Most folkloric collections do not have the tale types listed, so you may find this a very time-consuming and frustrating task. The most efficient way to locate the actual text of a story is to consult *A Guide to Folktales in the English Language* (based on the Aarne-Thompson Classification System) by D.L. Ashliman, where you will find the names of the stories that have the same plot, the title of the collections in which the stories appear, and even the page numbers the stories are on. Ashliman's book can also be accessed in reference and university libraries.

The next step is to gain some understanding of the tale type you have chosen, so you need to gather several stories of that type as samples. Pick a sample "telling" and look at Propp's list of actions. Try to recognize what actions drive the story forward and in which sequence. You may want to refer to Propp's book, *Morphology of the Folktale.* Remember, not all Propp's actions will be in the sample story. The 31 actions that Propp defined comprise a hypothetically "pure" fairy tale. Most of the tales we come across are not like that. They will have some of the Propp actions, but not all of them, and they may not be in the exact order. The story may start from the second, eleventh, or another action, and there will be omissions, additions, and repetitions.

When uncovering the structural bones of the story, strive to unearth the strongest bones, the purest version of the plot, and closest in form to the story's grass roots. You want to find the version unadulterated by writers and editors who skewed the plots and themes to their own purposes. This can be done by analyzing all the stories you gathered and then comparing them. After you list Propp's actions in each of the samples, you will be able to see any deviations, skips, and additions to the actions, and at which places they occurred. Basically, it will give you an understanding of your chosen tale type's flexibility and the boundaries that delineate its power. But you will find that the strongest bones are where the plots of the samples overlap, that is, the foundation of the tale type.

Once you find the story's bones, create a template of the tale type. You have a solid foundation that will hold and support countless new stories. Now construct the action-symbol map of the story, using the symbols from page 228 to 243, and develop guiding questions for creating a new story with your students.

Bibliography

Aarne, Antti. *The Types of the Folktale.* Translated and enlarged by Stith Thompson. Helsinki: Suomalainen Tiedeakatemia, 1873.

Applebee, Arthur N. *The Child's Concept of Story.* Chicago: The University of Chicago Press, 1978.

Ashliman, D.L. *A Guide to Folktales in the English Language: Based on the Aarne-Thompson Classification System.* New York: Greenwood Press, 1987.

Bettelheim, Bruno. *The Uses of Enchantment: The Meaning and Importance of Fairy Tales.* New York: Vintage Books, 1989.

Bosma, Bette. *Fairy Tales, Fables, Legends, and Myths: Using Folk Literature in Your Classroom.* New York: Teachers College Press, 1992.

Bruner, Jerome. *Acts of Meaning.* Cambridge, Massachusetts: Harvard University Press, 1990.

Chesterton, G.K. *"The Ethics of Elfland."* in *G.K. Chesterton: A Selection from His Non-fictional Prose.* Selected by W. H. Auden. London: Faber and Faber, 1970.

————. *The Man Who Was Orthodox.* London: Dennis Dobson, 1963.

Dreyfuss, Henry. *Symbol Sourcebook.* New York: John Wiley & Sons, 1984.

Edwards, Betty. *Drawing on the Right Side of the Brain.* New York: Jeremy P. Tarcher/Putnam, 1999.

Favat, André. *Child and Tale: The Origins of Interest.* Urbana: National Council of Teachers of English, 1977.

Franz, Marie-Louise von. *Archetypal Patterns in Fairy Tales.* Toronto: Inner City Books, 1997.

————. *The Interpretation of Fairy Tales.* Boston: Shambala, 1996.

Freed, Jeffrey and Laurie Parsons. *Right-Brained Children in a Left-Brained World.* New York: Simon & Schuster, 1998.

Gardner, Howard. *Artful Scribbles: The Significance of Children's Drawings.* New York: Basic Books, Inc. Publishers, 1980.

Hohr, Hansjorg. "Dynamic Aspects of Fairy Tales: Social and Emotional Competence through Fairy Tales." *Scandinavian Journal of Educational Research,* vol. 44, no. 1 (2002): 89–103.

Jenkins, Henry. "Game Design as Narrative Architecture." *First Person: New Media as Story, Performance, and Game,* eds. Noah Wardrip-Fruin and Pat Harrigan. Cambridge: MIT Press, 2004. 118–130.

Jones, Steven Swann. *The Fairy Tale: The Magic Mirror of the Imagination.* New York: Routledge, 2002.

Jung, Carl. *Four Archetypes: Mother/Rebirth/Spirit/Trickster.* Translated by R.F.C. Hall. Princeton: Princeton University Press, 1992.

————. *Man and His Symbols.* New York: Dell, 1968.

————. *The Psychology of the Transference.* Princeton: Princeton University Press, 1974

Lurie, Alison. *Clever Gretchen and Other Forgotten Folktales.* Illustrated by Margot Tomes. New York: Thomas Y. Crowell, 1980.

Luthi, Max. *Once Upon a Time: On the Nature of Fairy Tales.* Translated by Lee Chadeayne and Paul Gottwald. Bloomington: Indiana University Press, 1976.

————. *The Fairytale as Art Form and Portrait of Man.* Translated by Jon Erickson. Bloomington: Indiana University Press, 1984.

Pradl, Gordon M. *Narratology: The Study of Story Structure.* ERIC Digest. Urbana IL. 1984. Retrieved on-line June 1, 2008, at http://www.ericdigests.org/pre-921/story.htm.

Propp, Vladimir. *Morphology of the Folktale.* Translated by L. Scott and L.A. Wagner. Austin: University of Texas Press, 2001.

————. *Theory and History of Folklore.* Translated by Ariadna Y. Martin and Richard P. Martin. Edited by Anatoly Lieberman. Minneapolis: The University of Minnesota Press, 1984.

Rodari, Gianni. *The Grammar of Fantasy: An Introduction to the Art of Inventing Stories.* Translated by Jack Zipes. New York: Teachers & Writers Collaborative, 1996.

Rubright, Lynn. *Beyond the Beanstalk: Interdisciplinary Learning through Storytelling.* Portsmouth: Heinemann, 1996.

Segal, Lore, and Maurice Sendak, eds. *The Juniper Tree and Other Tales from Grimm.* New York: Farrar, Straus and Giroux, 1973.

Thomas, Joyce. *Inside the Wolf's Belly: Aspects of the Fairy Tale.* Worcester: Sheffield Academic Press, 1989.

Thompson, Stith. *The Folktale.* New York: The Dryden Press, 1951.

Tolkien, J.R.R. *Tree and Leaf.* London: Unwin Books, 1964.

Zipes, Jack. *Creative Storytelling: Building Community, Changing Lives.* New York: Routledge, 1995.

————. *Speaking Out: Storytelling and Creative Drama for Children.* New York: Routledge, 2004.

Notes to Chapters

Notes to Chapter 1

[1] Practical strategies for teaching children with Attention Deficit Disorder (ADD) are described in *Right-Brained Children in a Left-Brained World: Unlocking the Potential of Your ADD Child,* by Jeffrey Freed and Laurie Parsons (New York: Simon & Shuster, 1998).

Notes to Chapter 2

[2] J.R.R. Tolkien, *Tree and Leaf* (London: Unwin Books, 1964), 16.

[3] Joyce Thomas, *Inside the Wolf's Belly: Aspects of the Fairy Tale* (Worcester: Sheffield Academic Press, 1989), 90–91.

[4] G.K. Chesterton, *"The Ethics of Elfland."* in *G.K. Chesterton: A Selection from his Non-fictional Prose,* selected by W.H. Auden (London: Faber and Faber, 1970), 180.

[5] Tolkien, 20.

[6] Chesterton, *The Ethics of Elfland,* 181.

[7] Dr. Rupert Sheldrake, biologist and author, maintains that we all carry collective memories of our ancestors that he describes as an energy field. In Jungian psychology, the collective memories are viewed as archetypes.

[8] Thomas, 274–278.

[9] C.G. Chesterton, *The Man Who Was Orthodox* (London: Dennis Dobson, 1963), 175.

[10] Max Luthi, *The Fairytale as Art Form and Portrait of Man,* trans. Jon Erickson (Bloomington: Indiana University Press, 1984), 146.

[11] Thomas, 270, quoting Bettina Hurlimann, *Three Centuries of Children's Books in Europe,* trans. Brian W. Alderson (Cleveland: World, 1968), 21.

[12] The "listener" or "reader" implies both male and female.

[13] Thomas, 281, quoting James Hillman, "A Note on Story," *Children's Literature: The Great Excluded,* Vol. III (1972).

[14] Specifically, those were not animal stories, but stories with human heroes and magic.

[15] Nancy Davis, *Once Upon a Time, Therapeutic Stories that Teach and Heal* (Burke: Davis, 1996), v.

[16] Thomas, 281, quoting Hillman, "A Note on Story."

[17] With respect to folktales and children, there has been surprisingly little research done in a pedagogical setting. Among the few existing studies, Carol Bearse in 1992 and Elizabeth Yeoman in 1999 have looked into whether and how children use intertextual knowledge when writing their own stories. Ella Westland in 1993 explored children's responses to traditional versus fractured fairy tales, while more recently, Robin Mello's study in 2001 examined the impact of storytelling on children's self-concept. Three of these studies were conducted with children aged 9–13, perhaps to elicit more critically and verbally competent responses from the children. Bearse's, Yeoman's, and Mello's studies were limited to only one classroom of participants. Westland's study observed 100 participants.

Both Bearse and Yeoman concluded from their studies that children do indeed make intertextual links when writing their own stories. Also, their research illustrated that children create stories that disrupt traditional storylines of gender.

In a British study, Westland discovered the following: (a) In spite of the fact that many girls liked to paint princesses, they did not want themselves to be like princesses. The boys, on the other hand, liked the idea of being a prince. They saw it as being able to do what they wanted and spend lots of money (which outweighed the disadvantage of having to save and marry princesses). (b) The fractured fairy tales (with the independent heroines) were preferred by the girls, while no boys were interested in siding with sensitive non-standard heroes.

Mello's study suggested that storytelling impacts on students' interpersonal relationships, and enables the students to explore their own lives through the lens of the story. By participating in the storytelling, the children reflected on images and conditions in the story and linked them to known cultural concepts and paradigms and to their own life experiences.

The studies mentioned can be found in the following publications:

Westland, Ella. "Cinderella in the Classroom: Children's Responses to Gender Roles in Fairy-Tales." *Gender and Education* vol. 5, no. 3 (1993): 237–249;

Yeoman, Elizabeth. "How Does It Get Into My Imagination Elementary School Children's Intertextual Knowledge and Gendered Storylines." *Gender and Education* vol. 11, no. 4 (1999): 427–440;

Bearse, Carol I. "The Fairy Tale Connection in Children's Stories: Cinderella Meets Sleeping Beauty." *The Reading Teacher* vol. 45, no. 9 (May 1992): 687–694.

Mello, Robin. "The Power of Storytelling: How Oral Narrative Influences Children's Relationships in Classrooms." *International Journal of Education & the Arts* vol. 2, no.1, February 2001.

[18] Educator Kieran Egan also suggests that curriculum should be shaped like a story because it engages children's learning by tapping into their imaginations.

[19] Webster's New World Dictionary, 461.

Notes to Chapter 3

[20] Bruno Bettelheim, *The Uses of Enchantment: The Meaning and Importance of Fairy Tales* (New York: Vintage Books, 1989), 120.

[21] Archetypes are paradoxical in nature because they have both negative and positive aspects. Marie-Louise von Franz, a Jungian analyst and close associate of Jung, compared the archetypes to crystals. They are multi-faceted and we can approach them from different angles to obtain a variety of meanings and interpretations.

[22] A somewhat similar process can be found in Chinese metaphysics. Its foundation model, Yin-yang, contains patterns of *Po* and *Hun*, the two opposing forces. *Po* is the body power, while *Hun* is the dream spirit. The goal in Chinese medicine is to harmonize these two energies and bring them into balance. Only then can a person achieve self-realization.

23 C.G. Jung, *The Psychology of the Transference* (Princeton: Princeton University Press, 1974), 32, paragraph 396.

24 Favat drew on the following works of Jean Piaget: *The Language and Thought of the Child* (1955), *Judgment and Reasoning in the Child* (1968), *The Child's Conception of the World* (1967), and *The Moral Judgment of the Child* (1965).

   Piaget has often been criticized for this early work, with its subjective clinical procedures, small amounts of statistical evidence, and diffuse reporting. However, later studies by other researchers confirmed those findings and validated Piaget's work. Favat investigated further those criticisms, particularly the ones that applied to Piaget's studies of animism and the studies of moral development. Only then did Favat conclude that Piaget's work was invaluable to his research study and accepted it as a psychological reservoir of "children's characteristics."

   With respect to the studies of animism, Favat examined criticisms and works of Huang and Lee (1945), Strauss (1951), Klinberg (1957), and Russell (1940). Regarding the studies of moral development, Favat investigated the work of MacRae (1954), Durkin (1959a, 1959b), Loughran (1967), and Kohlberg (1963). All these researchers came to support Piaget's findings, and validation studies have confirmed the general hypothesis (Laurendeau and Pinard 1962; Gouin Decarie 1965; Elkin and Flavell 1969). More detailed description can be found in Andre Favat's work *Child and Tale: The Origins of Interest,* pp 20–24.

25 The "child" stands for both male and female.

26 Gianni Rodari, *The Grammar of Fantasy: An Introduction to the Art of Inventing Stories,* trans. Jack Zipes (New York: Teachers & Writers Collaborative, 1996), 48.

27 According to Piaget, fast forwarding the development will result in fragile learning.

Notes to Chapter 4

28 The "emergent curriculum" has become a concept of interest among many teachers in North America, and it is modelled on the principles and practices of the Reggio Emilia approach to early education in Italy.

29 Bettelheim, 121.

30 Betty Edwards, professor emeritus of art at California State University in Long Beach (who wrote and lectured about art, education, and the psychology of perception) noted that "Ideally, all information should be presented in at least two modes: verbal and pictographic." That is why I translated Propp's "actions" graphically into universal pictographs.

31 Howard Gardner, *Artful Scribbles: The Significance of Children's Drawing* (New York: Basic Books, Inc. Publishers, 1980), 152, quoting Alschuler and Hattwick from their study "Painting and Personality."

Notes to Chapter 5

32 Likely the children designated the squirrel as purple to make her magical. Purple is the most mystical of colours and it also denotes sorrow, making it a fitting indicator of both the creature's mystical quality and distress.

33 The imagery in video games is often derived from mythology and fairy tales. According to Jenkins, the games fit within a much older tradition of narratives such as heroes' odysseys and quest myths. Also in the same category could be included the works of J.R.R. Tolkien, Homer, and L. Frank Baum. While their knowledge of fairy tales and mythology was extensive and deep, the video game designers are mainly concerned with the mechanics of the game and often skip over the surfaces of the primary narratives. As a result, some of the fairy tale and mythology elements the designers employ in the computer video games carry distorted meaning. The child-players become recipients of a second-hand mythology, one that has been altered and processed by the game designers.

    For instance, one public school incident was unexpected when the children brought forth Golem as villain. In another public school, the children suggested a "good, cute dragon" for the magic helper in our story, which was another example of an altered symbol. The archetype of dragon carries both positive and negative meanings (as all archetypes do) and "symbolizes the primal energy upholding the material world, which can be turned to either good or evil purposes." Although in Asia the image of a dragon has emphasized its positive aspects, starting in the Christian era, in the West the dragon image has been relegated to represent evil, chaos, and destruction. The children's acquaintance with the Golem's and the dragon's altered meanings came primarily from the computer video games.

Jenkins suggests that, "… if game designers are going to tell stories they should tell them well. In order to do that, game designers, who are most often schooled in computer science or graphic design, need to be retooled in the basic vocabulary of narrative theory." One might add to it that they should familiarize themselves with the primal narratives as well, so that if they use their elements, they do so without distortion.

[34] By *newspaperman* the children meant a *newspaper delivery boy.*

[35] Rodari, 41.

Notes to Chapter 6

[36] Bettelheim, 106.

[37] These were personal observations based upon the students' lengthy and sophisticated written recollections and students' responses during the sessions. The observations were also supported by comments from the children's teachers.

[38] Bearse, Carol I. "The Fairy Tale Connection in Children's Stories: Cinderella Meets Sleeping Beauty." *The Reading Teacher* vol. 45, no. 9 (May 1992): 687–694.

[39] Yeoman, Elizabeth. "How Does It Get Into My Imagination Elementary School Children's Intertextual Knowledge and Gendered Storylines." *Gender and Education* vol. 11, no. 4 (1999): 427–440.

[40] Bettelheim, 279.

Notes to Chapter 7

[41] This is an example of a term no longer carrying meaning; it is a symbol that has died. The need to define the term would prove disruptive. However, utilizing the opportunity to define the term within the context of a fairy tale might make the fairy tale a powerful teaching tool in a history class for slightly older children.

[42] Bettelheim, 144, quoting Chesterton.

[43] Favat, 33, quoting Piaget.

[44] Gordon M. Pradl, "Narratology: The study of Story Structure," ERIC Digest, ED250698, 1984.

[45] To put such a recommendation into practice would require that teachers learn strategies for how to acknowledge the students' efforts.

Notes to Chapter 9

[46] Gardner, 149.

[47] Edwards, 39.

Acknowledgments

This book began as my graduate thesis, a quest to find out whether contemporary children could liberate folktales from their fixed form and take ownership by recreating them. That journey was so exciting, revealing and full of surprises that I just kept going longer after the initial research was finished. Along the way, there were many people who helped, listened and contributed in various ways. I'm very grateful to them all.

Carole Carpenter, a folklorist and an educator, guided me throughout my research at York University. She offered her generous advice and encouragement when I needed them, and became a dear friend. Thanks also to Leesa Fawcett and Isabel Killoran, my other advisors.

Vangelia Nitsis, a teacher-librarian, sparked my desire to embark upon my journey with children and fairy tales when I saw the work she did with one of my books and her students.

Sincere thanks to all of the primary teachers and librarians who opened the doors to their classrooms and allowed me to work with their students; in particular, to Gina Rhee, who showed me how easy it can be to adapt my approach within the classroom. As well, thanks goes to the students themselves, for their participation in my research and for allowing me to keep their drawings for further study.

Publisher Sharon Fitzhenry heard about the research I did with stories and children and suggested that I write a book about it for the educators, thus sending me further along on my quest.

Jeffrey Canton, a colleague and good friend always willing to hear about my latest discoveries, and Mary-Jane Moreau, teacher extraordinaire, both read through the early manuscript draft and offered their insights and helpful suggestions.

Michael Byron Davis, my editor, kept me on track and patiently helped to shape the manuscript with his sharp observations and comments.

Copy editor Jean Stinson encouraged me to re-visit my sentences and make them more concise.

Betsy Hearne, an award-winning educator, a writer, a reviewer and a folklorist whom I greatly respect and admire, read carefully through the final manuscript and put it into perspective with her foreword.

Finally, I want to thank David and Alexandra Charles, who coped with my fairy tales obsession for many years, and who helped me in countless ways, while I was researching and writing this book.